IT'S ALL ABOUT
HÍM

Hope for the desperate in Colombia

KATHLEEN KEITH-GILLON

WILD SIDE DESIGN

wildsidedesign.net

Kathleen Keith-Gillon
Email: katalina.keith@gmail.com

© 2017 Kathleen Keith-Gillon

Some sub-headings used in this book have been taken from sermons.

Written and published by:
Kathleen Keith-Gillon
Foreword by: Sefton Marshall
Print management:
Wild Side Publishing -
wildsidepublishing.com
Cover design:
Wild Side Design -
wildsidedesign.net

Cataloguing in Publication Data:
Title: It's All About Him
ISBN: 978-958-48-2195-9 (pbk.)
ISBN: 978-958-48-2339-7 (ePub)
Subjects: Memoir, Autobiography,
Christian Living

International distribution
Ingram Spark

CONTENTS

CONTENTS
(cont'd)

CONTENTS
(cont'd)

This is what normal Christianity looks like...
love poured out, unshakeable faith, unquestioning
obedience with signs and wonders following.

A stunning, true-life adventure of perseverance and life-
changing miracles experienced walking alongside the
broken and desperate in Colombia. A real faith-builder,
and an excellent discipleship and evangelistic tool.

Janet Balcombe
author *The Wild Side* and *Radical Lives* series

DEDICATION

I dedicate this book to all of you who have walked
alongside my sister and me, since we arrived in
Colombia in 1979. Your prayers and support bless us.
I dedicate this book to you Anita, my sister, friend and
partner in the ministry. You are an inspiration.

I leave as a spiritual legacy, unique treasures revealed to
me by my Heavenly Father. These I share in the section
entitled, *It's All About Him.*

FOREWORD

Several features contributed to the nervousness we were experiencing. We couldn't speak Spanish, and worse still, when we had told friends in NZ we were visiting Colombia, two of them responded with stories of being forcibly robbed while they were there. Perhaps you can imagine the comfort God's Spirit brought to us when we read the Colombian Tourist Bureau's promotion slogan, emblazoned across a wall in Bogotá Airport, 'The only risk is, you'll not want to leave!' They were so right!

Such was the start of the time for Claire and me when we visited Kathleen and Anita in Armenia, back in 2009. And how glad we were to see their welcoming faces and exuberant waving as we came through their local airport. We so enjoyed our time together.

Kathleen has a wonderful style of writing. Over the years I've come to appreciate the way she has written of people who have come to their door for spiritual help and encouragement. People from all walks of life. People with all sorts of needs. People who know they will be heard in a compassionate, Christ-like way by Anita and Kathleen. People who are seeking to be delivered from their situation, looking for freedom from what binds them.

These people are introduced to Jesus. The truth contained in Bible verses is spoken over them and used in prayers for them. The impact and significance of His death at Calvary is explained. The healing power of God's forgiveness through Him is emphasised. It's all about Him!

Here we have a collection of these events. Stories of real people, real situations, of real encounters, skilfully woven around stories of the Bible, all explaining God's forgiveness and healing. Like me,

I'm sure you'll be captivated by those stories. And more than that, I believe you'll capture afresh a glimpse of who God is, and how He brings victory to each of us.

The only risk is, you won't want to put this book down!

Sefton Marshall
Operations Director
Global Connections in Mission (GC3)
Palmerston North, New Zealand
September 2017

HIS PLAN

"For I know the plans I have for you," declares the LORD,
"plans to prosper you and not to harm you,
plans to give you hope and a future."

Jeremiah 29:11

THREE DESTINATIONS — ONE DIVINE PLAN

Washing and watching. Watching and washing. She squeezed the water out of the tiny jacket and glanced down at her premature firstborn in the basket. Then she hung the garment on the line, and contented, sat down to watch over the clothes and her baby.

It was February 1949. The *S S Maloja* was sailing from Bombay to the South Pacific. India had been Mary's home. A career woman, fulfilled and happy in her job, she had not anticipated marriage, until she met Geoffrey.

Mary smiled. Reaching down, she gently turned back the blanket and took her sleeping daughter tenderly in her arms. She smiled again as she thought of the future. A new life; a new land. Their baby would thrive in New Zealand.

*** *** ***

Acts 17:26 tells us that God determines the times set for us, and the exact places where we should live. We can be sure that His plans are always for our good.

Jeremiah 29:11 assures us that they are plans to prosper us and not to harm us. Plans to give us hope and a future.

The baby did thrive. My parents found life in New Zealand exceeded their expectations, and within a few months, I was plump and healthy.

*** *** ***

On Christmas Day 1973, twenty-four years later, I leaned on the rail of the *RHMS Ellinis* as she ploughed her way across the Atlantic Ocean. A magnificent rainbow stretched from port to starboard. I lowered my camera and smiled. Our rainbow; put there by God to remind us He always keeps His promises.

As I stood gazing at how the rainbow's colours merged with the dark blue water, my thoughts went back to our frantic last days in New Zealand. About to step out from under the protective umbrella of a Christian home, my sister and I made our own special prayer request. We had asked God to give us Christian friends on our month-long voyage to England.

The ship's programme sheet, slipped under our cabin door some time during each night, advertised a Bible study group. Curious to fellowship outside our church circle, we immediately joined the group. Our prayer was answered. Our new friends were a young Australian couple with four small children, who provided us with hours of entertainment. We missed them when they disembarked in Panama, before heading down to begin missionary work in Colombia.

The rainbow gradually faded. I shivered and slipped my camera into its case. I would treasure that snapshot. Awesome evidence that our God had kept His promise to His two children: the promise to hear and to answer. *"The Lord will hear when I call to Him"* (Psalm 4:3). David was sure of it, and I echoed his words in Psalm 66:19. *"God has surely listened and heard my voice in prayer."*

Ahead lay a new life, in a new land. I stared out across the horizon. Tomorrow we would reach the Azores. Next week we would be in England.

*** *** ***

God has a plan for our lives and His plans stand firm forever (Psalm 33:11). Nothing happens by chance in the lives of His children.

On October 12, 1978, the haunting strains of a lone bugle on the wharf side were drowned by a burst of song from the multi-racial crowd on the deck of the *MV Doulos*. I snapped a photo of the bugle player and then joined in the singing. London disappeared into the fog, as our ship slowly moved down the River Thames.

Fine cuisine and the good service of attentive Greek stewards on the *RHMS Ellinis* were our memories of life at sea. The *Doulos* did not carry pampered passengers. A breakfast announcement brought this home. "Sorry, there is no tea to drink. The steam has shut down." Could we English survive? We did.

We quickly learned that one of the ship's ministries is to teach Christians to live out their Christianity in a multi-cultural environment. The German personnel manager assigned us to work in the ship's laundry. Our boss was an Indian fellow from Singapore, our co-workers, Malaysian, German and Taiwanese. Our work? Washing for the 269 people on board.

After our first day's work, I wrote home: "It's a steamy place. Most of the day we fed pink tablecloths and white sheets through a gigantic press."

Ten days later, we experienced the full force of a storm near the Azores. Five years previously, I had photographed a rainbow in these waters. Now the sea was green-grey and heaving. The horizon tilted alarmingly. Our boss closed the laundry. I wrote: "By afternoon it was too rough to stand up in there."

The knowledge that God knows the end from the beginning (Isaiah 46:10), is reassuring in the middle of a storm. We were on our way to Colombia to join our missionary friends from the *RHMS Ellinis*.

Their frequent letters had awakened an interest in their work. They wrote asking us to pray for schoolteachers for their children and for those of another missionary couple. Through that letter, God spoke clearly and directly. "Go."

To a new life. To a new land.

The storm passed. The laundry re-opened, and for the next three and a half months, we carried on with the washing.

*** *** ***

"*'I know the plans I have for you,' says the Lord*" (Jeremiah 29:11). What security!

After almost 40 years of proving God's faithfulness to my sister and me, as missionaries in Colombia, almost 40 years of watching God's divine plan unfold, I echo the words of W. Trobish: "He has the film of my whole life in view, not just the snapshot of my present situation."

RED TAPE, GREEN MISSIONARIES

The veteran missionary leaned across the lunch table, distress stamped on his kind face. Mystified, I looked over at his wife. She averted her eyes, and shifted uneasily in her chair. A giant question mark hung in the air over our empty plates.

When he finally broke the awkward silence, Harvey's voice was strained.

"I gather no one has told you." He swallowed before hurrying on. "Your resident visas haven't been applied for yet. With the recent refusals, we thought it prudent to wait."

His words reached my ears, but did not penetrate the cotton wool inside my head. I struggled to comprehend.

My sister Anita, and I, had embarked on the Operation Mobilisation's ship *MV Doulos* in London 3½ months previously, totally convinced that the granting of our resident visas would coincide with our arrival in Colombia.

It hadn't. The news came as a shock. Because I didn't accept what I had just heard, I forgot to tell my sister until several hours later.

"Harvey told me they haven't applied for our visas."

Neither of us recorded this information, or our reaction to it, in our diaries on February 8, 1979. Why would we? We were in denial. For the rest of the crew, Barranquilla was just another port. As usual, the purser issued everyone with shore-passes, and so we accepted an invitation to stay on shore with Harvey and his wife, Ruth.

The following morning, I lay in bed and listened to the tropical birds calling to one another in the coconut palms outside my window — a pleasant change from the anguished cries of hungry seagulls.

I stretched luxuriously. Today there would be no ship's bells to respond to, no clothes to fold in the ship's laundry.

The smell of guavas and freshly made toast brought me back to the present. We were in Colombia. We had no visas.

What was to be done with us? The options were tossed round the breakfast table. Should we sail with the ship to Venezuela? Should we try for tourist visas?

"Count on us," promised Ruth. "We'll do all we can to help you."

Immediately after breakfast, we climbed into their ancient jeep for the first of many trips into town, 40 minutes' drive away.

The hot, dry wind whipped the clips out of our prim British hairstyles as we sped through the barren countryside.

This new life is going to knock the stuffiness out of us, I mused.

As if to confirm my thought, Ruth turned to where we sat in the back seat, and offered us a stick of American chewing gum. Next minute we were savouring the tart green-apple flavour and privately wondering why we'd never chewed gum before.

Harvey slowed as we approached the outskirts of the town, and we noticed long lines of people standing in the blazing sun.

"Water's rationed," Ruth informed us.

Looking more closely, we saw that everyone had brought a bucket or a tin. Skinny youths jostled with careworn women; small children, with old, pinched faces, squatted in the dirt. Further along the road, we passed a rusty tanker. An old man ladled out water, while a police officer tried to maintain order with a wooden truncheon.

Our first stop in town was at the Venezuelan consul's office.

An overweight man in a pale blue suit handed us some forms and indicated that we needed the British consul's signature. Back into the jeep we clambered, and drove to the British consulate. An impeccable Jamaican Englishman received us courteously, but informed us his government gave him no authority to sign the papers. He suggested we go to the *Doulos* shipping agent.

We began to get the feeling we were being shunted along – victims of a society where red tape twists itself around anyone who dares to challenge the system.

A rickety old bus swung drunkenly around the corner. The driver braked violently. We pushed our way on, and wriggled between the sweaty bodies jammed in the aisle. I found my face pushed under the armpit of a perspiring farm-worker who was hugging a squawking hen in a flimsy sack.

The driver leaned forward and peered from behind a fringe of psychedelic-pink woollen tassels, draped around the cracked windscreen. I hoped he could see where he was going, because I couldn't. I gave up trying and glanced down to see the road rushing along beneath my feet. Rust had eaten a hole in the floor.

Eventually we were catapulted into a crowd of people on a street corner. Carl, our guide, strode into a building, and whisked us up to the twelfth floor. Ushered into the manager's air-conditioned office, we were invited to sit round a highly polished table. First came the lengthy introductions and greetings, then our case was discussed.

"No hay problema."

The shipping agent assured us he could procure our tourist visas. He reached for his telephone and dialled the Foreign Office.

Our hopes soared, and then plummeted when he replaced the receiver and shook his head. We understood enough Spanish to gather that a new law no longer allowed tourist visas to be granted within the country. That this was news to the shipping agent baffled us, coming from England, a country where laws were as ancient and secure as the Magna Carta.

The secretary approached us with a silver tray bearing miniature china cups. We thought her most kind, and gratefully sipped the bitter-sweet black coffee. Later we would become accustomed to this service during business transactions. She began to type up a letter for us to take somewhere else.

Just as well Carl is helping us, I thought, as we'd lost our way in the maze of words and gesticulations.

By the time we eventually left the air-conditioned office and stepped out into the midday heat, everything was beginning to shut down for the two-hour siesta period. What we didn't get done today, would now wait until 'mañana'.

That afternoon, I lay in the hammock and read through the first newsletter we'd sent out before leaving England:

"What God has not yet shown us, is when our visas will come. We know we cannot enter Colombia without them, but our God is a God of miracles. We believe our visas will be granted and that God will receive all the glory."

I closed my eyes and tried to straighten out my confused thoughts. Our arrival in Colombia had been an anti-climax. God had not worked things out the way we had anticipated when we took the enormous step of faith, and embarked on the Doulos.

We had been so sure. More than once on the voyage, promises from God had blazed out of Bible passages we'd read.

In mid-January it was: *"Your faith is large and your request is granted"* (Matthew 15:28 TLB).

A week later: *"Trust in the Lord and do good so shalt thou dwell in the land"* (Psalm 37:3 KJV).

Ouch! I opened my eyes and slapped a mosquito on my leg. Hey, we *were* in the land. We'd entered Colombia *without* visas. Now that really was a miracle!

I scribbled the opening sentence to the letter our prayer partners were waiting for: "Here we are in Colombia (without our visas) because our God is a God of miracles."

I paused, suddenly feeling small and insignificant. My frustration at being entangled in red tape subsided. We were not victims. We were protagonists in an ongoing miracle-drama. The director was none other than God Himself.

Our next step, to get Venezuelan visas, was straight forward. It was an 'if all else fails' move and this didn't do credit to our faith. We stood in lines, filled in forms, and had our fingerprints taken. The official stamped the visas in our passports. Now, if all else failed, we could go on to Venezuela with the mission ship.

So far, all queries about tourist visas had been met with a negative response. But one afternoon, Harvey stopped the jeep outside the Foreign Office. We sat and waited. Waiting is a major part of life in Colombia. He came out with a half-smile.

"Been talking about you," he said, as he settled himself behind the steering wheel. "The fellow says to take your passports in on Monday. They'll see what they can do." Obviously he'd been speaking to a different person. We learned another mystery of Colombian culture: "No" doesn't necessarily mean "no".

Monday saw us climbing into the old jeep once more. We wound down the windows and let the hot dust-laden wind blow into our faces. Anything to get cool. The vehicle bumped its way along the unpaved tracks of a shantytown. Folk stopped and stared at us; half-naked children ran out of the shacks made of cardboard and sheets of tin. We waved and they grinned. Then we turned down a tree-lined street, where armed guards stood outside the mansions of the rich, where maids in crisp uniforms swept the footpath and pushed plump babies in fancy strollers. The great disparity between the wealthy and the poor staggered us. At the Foreign Office, we handed our passports to Harvey, and sat down to wait. I balanced my writing pad on my knee and began a letter home:

"I am sitting in the Oficina Extranjera, i.e. the Foreign Office. The next few moments are crucial. But then every moment seems that way just now."

We accomplished little that morning. Just another visit to the shipping agent to ask for another letter. Then followed another night of waiting and praying. Another trip into town.

The official read the letter. To this day, we have no idea of its contents. Was it palanca — that ingredient of Latin American life where, "Who you know is more important than what you know"? Maybe.

The man scrutinised our passports, pausing every now and then to copy down some detail. He then produced an inkpad and asked for our thumb and index fingerprints, before handing everything to his senior.

In a few minutes, the suspense was over and we had our passports back in our hands. The ink was still wet. The visa read:

"Puede permanecer 90 días."

"You can stay 90 days," Harvey translated. He and Ruth were both astounded.

"Could've been 15 days, with an order that you can't ask for an extension," marvelled Ruth.

*** *** ***

The veteran missionary pushed aside his empty plate and leaned back in his chair. His face creased into a satisfied smile. I looked across at his wife and her eyes met mine. There was a comfortable silence — the kind only felt among good friends.

Finally Harvey spoke: "Let's make a start on the paper work to apply for your resident visas."

RED TAPE, WHITE KNUCKLES

"I hate these beastly restrictions."

The metal edge of the window ledge dug into my elbows. As I shifted my position, I realised my hands were tightly clenched.

In a matter of days, our 90-day visas would expire. If the authorities refused to give us an extension, we'd have to leave Colombia.

I made a conscious effort to relax and cupped my chin in my hands. Kneeling on the bed beside me, my sister put words to my thoughts. Frustration added a metallic edge to her voice.

"I'm beginning to wonder if we'll ever get residency here."

Together, we looked out over the tops of the banana plants. The enormous floppy leaves, silver in the moonlight, flapped gently. A moth fluttered over our heads into the bedroom. With the cicadas providing the background music, the magic of the tropical night gradually soothed our frazzled spirits.

I switched off the light and we lay in our beds reliving the past three months. We recalled the jubilant feeling we experienced when we received our 90-day visas.

Right now, 90 days didn't seem such a wonderful figure.

"Could all they asked for, really be necessary to get our resident visas?"

My sister's question fluttered like an ungainly moth in the darkness. I felt my fingers tighten round my thumbs.

Still no sign of our resident visas. It was obvious we would have to apply for an extension on our tourist visas.

"What if they don't give us an extension?"

The awful thought hit us. I watched a beetle hitting itself against the window pane. I understood its frustration.

"What if we have to leave the county? What if ..."

The fluorescent beetle circled the bedroom before drifting out the window. A hundred what-ifs circled round in our heads. Eventually we drifted off to sleep.

A deluge of encouragement

The next few days brought a deluge of encouragement from the Scriptures. The devotional book, Living Light, gave a refreshing slant on well-known verses.

"I want you to be free from worry. Don't worry about anything. Tell God your needs and don't forget to thank Him for His answers. If you do this you will experience God's peace which is far more wonderful than the human mind can understand" (Philippians 4:6-7 LB).

Peace

The message came across clearly. A couple of days later we read: *"All who fear God and trust in Him are blest beyond expression. Such a man will not be overthrown by evil circumstances. God's constant care of Him will make a deep impression on all who see it. He does not fear bad news nor live in dread of what may happen. For he is settled in his mind that Jehovah will take care of him"* (Psalm 112:1, 6, 7 TLB).

Constant care – We felt comforted

Life continued as normal. We helped in the orphanage in the mornings. We studied the Spanish language up in our little bedroom in the afternoons. But that uncertain, unsettled feeling was there all the time.

We might fly up to the capital in two days' time, but would seats be available at such short notice? We might not be given a visa extension. Maybe we'd have to leave the country. Should we pack for an overnight stay, when we went up to apply for our extension, or should we take enough for several months?

Then we read the following comment by J.R. McDuff on James 4:6: *"He giveth more grace. God does not give grace till the hour of trial comes. But when it does come, the amount of grace and the nature of the special grace required is kindly dispensed. Do not perplex yourself with what is needed for future emergencies; tomorrow will bring its promised grace hand in hand with tomorrow's trials."*

Grace for all our tomorrows

Thank you, Lord.

The old black telephone shrilled, and the travel agent's secretary spoke.

"We have two cancellations. We can offer you two seats on tomorrow's flight."

The phone rang again. The missionary in Bogotá had heartening news.

"Yes, you can stay at our place, and I'll help you with the legal business at the office."

As a special extra, God threw a rainbow across the stormy sky, as we drove into town to buy our plane tickets. A thrilling, visible sign of His infallibility.

Suddenly, we stopped quivering on the cliff edge clutching our what-ifs, mights and maybes and flung ourselves into space. Borne by the parachute of God's promises, we soared above our worries.

With overnight bags, we flew up to Bogotá next day, in brilliant sunshine.

Another tangle

As he promised, our new friend Brian, accompanied us downtown. We rode the lift to a fourth floor office, only to find ourselves in another tangle of red tape. There are complicated steps to every transaction in Colombia.

"Your solicitude please." The secretary snapped her fingers.

Whatever it was, we didn't have it.

The girl haughtily pointed to the door with her chin. Big white plastic beads bounced on her bosom, as she waved her arms about and broke into a torrent of Spanish. Mesmerised, we stared blankly. Our guide assured us all was OK, and hurried us out to the elevator.

Outside on the footpath, he pointed to a row of little men. Each sat in front of an ancient typewriter, balanced on a rickety, wooden table. We approached one, whose face reminded me of a wrinkled prune. Cheap cologne did a poor job of disguising his peculiar odour. My sister, a typewriting teacher, gave his dilapidated typewriter a withering glance.

"An application form for a visa extension, please." Brian briefly gave him the details and they negotiated a price.

The wizened old fellow dropped his cigarette and squashed it with his foot. Methodically, he thumped the keys. I noticed one of his fingers was missing. He thumped slowly - too slowly.

I glanced at my watch and wrapped my fingers tightly round my thumbs. We were running out of time.

Handing over our fee, we took the paper and raced back to the office. It was closing time.

"Come back next Wednesday."

The secretary barely glanced at our precious application form. She put it with a pile of papers on top of her filing cabinet, and turned back to the little mirror in her hand. We left her putting the finishing touches to her red lips.

Next day we checked that Brian could sign for and collect our promised visa extensions. All was in order. Highly elated, we floated down the road to celebrate at a chicken eating-house.

Visa extension

The authorities gave us 30 days — our countdown to leave the country. We had 30 days to make inquiries, plans, decisions.

On Day 22, a letter arrived from Costa Rica. I ripped open the envelope and scanned the contents.

"We've been accepted for language school," I chirped excitedly. "Hey, classes begin on the 28th. We leave here on the 20th. How's that for perfect timing?"

But right now it was a race against time. Student visas for Costa Rica, money for our airfares, flight connections.

On the thirtieth day of our 30 day extension, we snapped our suitcases shut, fastened our seatbelts and flew out to Costa Rica.

More red tape

Three months later, a letter from Colombia brought good news.

"I have in my possession the authorised copies of the visas (one for Kathleen and one for Anita). You have to present these copies in San Antonio del Táchira in order to be able to claim the visas there."

We had an important question for the Colombian consul in Costa Rica. Carefully we constructed the short sentence in perfect Spanish.

"Necesitamos visas para entrar a Colombia?"

"Oh no," he reassured us. "You are travelling on British passports, so you don't need visas to enter Colombia."[1]

But as our plane circled the Barranquilla airport before nosing down towards the runway, niggling doubts wriggled around in our minds. Had we been too trusting? Had we understood the consul's reply? Involuntarily my fingers closed tightly over my thumbs as we threaded our way through the building to the immigration desk. The official flipped over the pages of our passports. He raised his bushy eyebrows and adjusted his glasses.

"You've already had three months in Colombia this year," he barked.

I groaned inwardly. *More red tape?* No one had told us that three months was the limit to be in Colombia on a British passport.

"I'll give you 24 hours," he snapped. "You can get an eight-day extension at our downtown office tomorrow morning. Of course there'll be a fine to pay," he concluded.

Ouch! It hurt to part with money for a fine.

After three exhausting trips to the immigration office, we eventually got our 8 days permission.

On the seventh day, we flew to Cucuta. Our good guide Carl met us and drove us the nine kilometres to San Antonio just over the Venezuelan border.

Five fifteen that afternoon found us sitting in the dim coolness

---

1 We travelled on British passports because our parents were British

of the consul's office. I clenched my hands together and studied my white knuckles. The only sound came from the whirring of the enormous ceiling fan.

The consul's lemon-yellow shirt barely stretched across his paunch. He blinked his owl-like eyes and lethargically reached for our passports.

His nail-polish glistened in the half light, as slowly and deliberately he picked up an expensive-looking fountain pen.

He gave us visas for two years.

As we shook hands, I felt sorry for him. He had no idea of the significance of the moment.

Anti-climax

Our next experience was an anti-climax. Out at the Cucuta airport next morning, we bounced up to the desk and triumphantly presented our passports.

"You can't travel."

We shrivelled under the policewoman's stony stare. She sniffed, and proceeded to spit out our crimes.

"You didn't register when you left Colombia for San Antonio yesterday. You didn't register on re-entry."

With a wave of the hand, she coldly dismissed us to their downtown office to pay a fine, and get our papers in order.

Deflated we slunk out of the airport.

No restrictions

Two years passed. Time to apply for our permanent visas. Time to visit our parents in New Zealand.

Tension mounted.

"You can't apply until your two-year visas actually expire," the travel agent informed us.

We checked our departure dates. The flight home to New Zealand was scheduled to leave three days after our visa expiry date. We were back on the cliff edge, hovering, while we waited for a hitch in obtaining US visas to be ironed out.

The Lord quietened our agitated hearts with His gentle voice:

"I will never leave you or forsake you" (Joshua 1:5).

Barely three hours before our flight to Bogotá, the travel agent phoned through our visa confirmation. Wow! That was too close for comfort.

An electrical storm had the 16-seater Fokker bucking and bouncing over the Andes Mountains. We were still tense when we arrived in Bogotá 40 minutes later, to pick up our visas.

"Your passports aren't ready yet."

The words splashed colder than the rain that splashed on our faces, as we hurried to the taxi stand.

Not ready? But we leave for New Zealand tomorrow morning. Panic threatened to take over.

What if ... what if... what if.... My thoughts swished back and forth in time with the windscreen wipers.

We headed straight to the travel agency, marched in and sat down. We waited. We watched the clock.

5.00 p.m. ...

5.10 p.m. ...

5.15 p.m. ...

5.20 p.m. ...

A man in a dark suit appeared. He held our passports. I unclasped my hands to receive mine. Feverishly, I flicked through until I found the permanent visa stamp. The all-important word was handwritten in black ink: Indefinida.

We have no restrictions on the length of our residency in Colombia.

EVERYTHING HAS A BEGINNING
A piece of history

Usually a major project on the mission field is only put into action after a lot of careful thought and planning. For us, this was not so.

There were no plans, except, of course, in the heart of God, with whom we communicated every move, and confided every idea. In February 1979 when we arrived in Colombia on board the *MV Doulos,* we had no idea that one day we would be mother figures to 16+ children.

For our first five years in Colombia, we were responsible for the school education of seven Australian children, during which time we used our beginner's Spanish, teaching children's Bible classes on a Saturday afternoon. Apart from the Sunday services this was our only contact with Colombians.

In 1984 we moved from the farm, where we had been teaching missionaries' children, to live in the city of Armenia; we began to have more contact with Colombians there. One family in particular concerned us — a young couple in the church where we worshipped, had six small children suffering from malnutrition. We felt this was a disgrace to the testimony of the local church, so we, and two of the elders, made ourselves responsible for the four eldest, who were in a more serious condition than the younger ones.

Jody* was six years old; his weight, 12 kilos, and his height that of a three-year-old. The paediatrician advised us to take him under our care while he recovered, and explained that his basic need was to receive love. And so it proved. During the nine years we cared for him, first like a sponge, then like a leech, he demanded our full attention every waking hour. His family situation gradually worsened and within a few months collapsed completely. We received his brothers, Jeff and Joe, and Dave the seventh child, was also with us for a short time. With these four little boys, we moved to a house with a big back yard.

One day, there was a knock at the door. A young woman, who had seen us out walking with our little brood, brought us her five-year-old daughter to look after. Alexa lived with us until she was a teenager. Then 18-month-old Sue came for temporary care while her mother was in hospital, followed by Leanne and Eunice both under two years old. They were daycare children.

The following year, when Eddy arrived, and Sue came back with her six-year-old brother, Alf, we began to think and pray about buying a big house. After walking round dozens of suburbs and looking over numerous houses, we found one. The only problem was, we didn't have enough money to buy it. However, the owner was willing to rent it to us for six months. When he put it up for sale again, he asked almost twice the original price. We explained our unique situation, i.e. no regular income, and to our amazement, he accepted our unusual terms, to pay what we could, when we could, no doubt thinking of the interest money he expected to receive for a long time. To God be the glory, the house was paid off in five months.

Ten-year-old Judy was the first increase in the family in our new home. She came from a brothel run by her mother. In 1988, we received Dior, a five-year-old intellectually and physically handicapped boy, and Anna a three-year-old abandoned by her mother and neglected by her father. Then, there was Allie, a ten-year-old, brought by a lady in the church fellowship. Shortly after her arrival, we found out she had been having treatment for leukaemia, but that her mother had suspended it. We re-initiated the treatment and God healed her. Carl, seven, and his 11-month-old sister were brought to us just when we'd decided that six boys and six girls were a nice, complete family. Cody, also 11 months' old was brought to us for day care, but his deplorable home situation made full time care a necessity.

In March the following year, Jeff walked out after we caught him stealing, and his place was immediately taken by a badly nourished six-year-old, Paul. His mother had been pleading for help every week or so, for several months, but we'd had no bed for him. Jeff's departure was the answer to her prayer.

There were other children: Freddy, a daycare child who was repeatedly left with us overnight; Mary, our first and only child of African descent; Monty, a five-year-old, who cried so much, we had to set aside a special chair where he could sit when overcome with grief; Jonny, a ten-year-old, who had started First Grade four times, and never finished, because his mother moved house so frequently; Xavier, seven years old, so over-protected that he didn't know how to play. He broke his arm after a week with us. An unforgettable afternoon was spent with a South American Indian man, trying to convince him that we couldn't take his little daughter. He wouldn't take no for an answer; he'd brought Paulina to stay. Melva joined the family in early 1990. A few days later, a teacher from the local school begged us to take one of her pupils, so Astrid came by the day until she could be squeezed in.

Barely a week later, Norah and Minnie, 13-year-old twins, turned our world upside down. Their arrival caused jealousy. Orphaned only a few days earlier, they needed special care, understanding, and literally hours of our time. The other children interpreted this attention as favouritism. The atmosphere became tense and we had to find another home for Minnie. We tried again nine months later, treating her and Judy as equally as possible, but Judy's behaviour deteriorated to such an extent that it was almost a relief when she announced that she wanted to leave us, and try out a different life style.

At this time, Jeff was living with his father. He would visit us for help with homework, but he stole a large sum of money from us, so we couldn't have him back to visit.

Lana arrived in 1993. We weren't going to take any more children, but hers was a case of mental abuse. Then out of the blue, Jonny, now a teenager, reappeared and begged to stay. He had run away from his home. Unfortunately, he was unable to keep even the most elementary rules, which meant our teenage girls were not safe with him in the home. After a month, we handed him over to his mother.

That same day, Jody dropped his bombshell. He told us that it had been nice living with us, but that he had decided to leave. We made it clear that he would leave without our permission, but neither would we stop him, and took the precaution of telling him exactly what kind of life he was choosing. His mind was made up; he packed his bags and left. Because of his rebellious and consequently disruptive behaviour over a long period, his leaving was something of a relief, but on the other hand, it was a painful experience because we knew he was choosing to live with thieves, prostitutes and drug dealers, and that for most of the time, he'd be living on the streets. We think back to the day when, as a six-year-old, he interrupted an explanation of the Gospel, and pled with God to forgive his sins. Only the Father knows what really took place in his heart, and although his life is now a mess, we claim God's keeping power for him.

It was because of Jody's need, that the Home came into existence. His rejection of years of love has helped us to see things more from God's point of view. Are we here to count successes and commiserate over failures? What of Jeff, who hasn't been heard of again? Jonny, has he gone back to gang warfare in Medellin? And Judy, who went to live with the 17-year-old father of her baby? Why didn't she listen to our advice and benefit from our counsel?

All these experiences have helped us to establish our goals, and recognise that God is not so much interested in what we are doing for Him, as in what He is doing in us. The 44 children, who were in our care at different times during those 11 years, have played a part in bringing about His purposes in our lives. We learnt patience by hard experience; we have empathy with the parents of rebellious teenagers; we have gained a deeper understanding of the Colombian culture and find we have a greater acceptance with the people because we have faced the same struggles; although single, we can speak with authority on many family issues.

We provided a Christian environment for underprivileged children, from dysfunctional homes, where they were all given the opportunity to choose God's way. Some did, some didn't.

I am looking at a powerful statement from the book of Joshua. It is in Gothic lettering over an archway in our living room.

"As for me and my household, we will serve the Lord" (Joshua 24:15).

We have taken it as a prophetic statement over all the children who have lived with us, as part of our family. *"They <u>will</u> serve the Lord"*.

Although we may not see the fulfilment of that promise in our lifetime, one day they will serve the Lord. Our faith in that statement encourages us to keep on praying and to keep on loving them, the spouses they have chosen and their children who call us Grandma.

All names have been changed to protect the identity of the children.

COLOMBIAN
KALEIDOSCOPE

That in all things He might have the pre-eminence.

Colossians 1:18 (AKJV)

COLOMBIAN KALEIDOSCOPE

During a visit to our home you may encounter drug addicts, prostitutes, drug-lords, New-agers, ex-guerrillas, ex-paramilitary, ex-gang leaders, Satanists, homosexuals, lesbians, Catholics, evangelical pastors, divorcees, ex-wives of drug-lords, rebellious teenagers, rapists and people who have made multiple attempts at suicide.

My sister Anita and I have a counselling, teaching and mentoring ministry in the town of Armenia, Colombia.

What is the answer to the many and varied situations we face?

We are quite clear. The answer is Christ. **It's all about Him.**

So why do people come to our home? They are people in crisis looking for answers. Pastors send us their hopeless cases; headmasters refer their difficult pupils to us. People on the verge of suicide, phone us. Quarrelling couples arrive together, but refuse to look at one another. Everyone who comes is left in no doubt that the only answer to his or her problem is Jesus Christ. **It's all about Him.**

The spiritual needs of pastors and Christian leaders take priority. When coming from other areas, we receive them in our home. Hospitality is an integral part of the ministry. Often, some of the most important conversations are held over a meal.

COMINGS AND GOINGS

Visit us and wander round. Don't be shy; feel free to ask who all these folk are!

Friday

Who are all those people in the lounge? It's a bit early for visitors. Oh, they are pastors who have come together to discuss a project, and they chose to meet in our house, so as to be on neutral ground.

Who's the man upstairs on the landing, ironing his shirt? That's John*. He's staying here, while in a restoration process.

Do I recognise the two scruffy looking fellows having lunch in the dining room? One seems familiar. Oh, one is our son, Alf. He and his brother-in-law have come to Armenia to work at painting and decorating this week. Excuse their grubby clothes.

Who are those two school boys? I've never seen them here before. They come every Friday for lunch and for help with their English homework.

Talking of English, do I imagine it, or are those two young ladies in the back court yard, talking in English? Yes, the blonde one is Allie, who comes to stay with us every Friday through Sunday, and her friend is here on a visit this week. They are from the United States. Allie is in Armenia for her gap year, teaching English at a Christian college.

Saturday

A lame man just came in without ringing the doorbell. Is he known to you? Yes. He's Victor; he comes by most days to break his long walk and read the newspaper.

There's a lady at the door. Shall I let her in? Of course. She's Christy, who has come to pray the Word of God for an hour, with Kathleen.

The lounge is full again. Who are all these people? Oh, they are a group who meet in our house every Saturday afternoon. Anita has been invited to teach the workshop, *Freedom from Bitterness*.

Do I hear children's voices upstairs? You sure do. Our granddaughters, Annabelle and Mary Jane, are staying this weekend.

And what about the teenage boy I met on the stairs with Anita just now? Oh, that's Val's son, Stephen, who asked for an urgent appointment. He'd seen a horrifying film at school and wanted to pray about the effect it was having on his spiritual life.

Sunday

Who's the tall, silver-haired gentleman in the kitchen? He's Harvey. He's here in a restoration process. He's preparing breakfast for us all.

It is nice to see all the adult children here for lunch today. I counted 10 or was it 12? The fact they come in bit by bit, stretches lunch over a long time, doesn't it? And there was a girl I didn't recognise. She was Alf's brother-in-law's girlfriend. Don't worry, we didn't know her either.

What a blessing the majority of your children had left this afternoon before that couple arrived to visit you. Who were they? Oh, our friendship with them goes back for almost 30 years. We were enjoying a catch-up.

Who are these two pretty teenage girls who have just rushed into the house and hugged you so ecstatically? They are Nina and Sally, Greg's girls, come by for Nina's birthday present.

Oh no, not another visitor? Can you cope? Don't worry, he's Joe's father and we'll leave Joe to rustle up something for him to eat. I'm going upstairs to write to our prayer partners!

ONE OF THE FAMILY

Victor limped into our lives in the mid-nineties, one of the many 'all alone in this world' people. His marriage was a long forgotten affair and there were no children. He adopted us as his family and we sometimes think of him as our eldest son.

Stricken with polio in the early 1950s, he only managed to complete two years of primary school; study for him was not an option. Before his eleventh birthday, he was learning the metalwork trade, in order to support himself and his mother. Life had not been kind to Victor, and when we first knew him, he was bitter and off side with everyone.

In 2010, he heard of a chaplaincy course, but with barely two years of primary school, could he meet the entry requirements? Somehow he did. The theological studies, Bible-study courses and his years of experience as a prison visitor were in his favour.

It was a great disappointment, when after completing the course, he found himself on the bottom rung of the ladder. He could not advance without his secondary school certificate. But instead of deterring him, this challenged him to go back to school. Every Saturday afternoon for the next three years, he attended classes for adults; every night of the week he pored over his books, filled in the exercises, and struggled with math.

His high-school graduation was a triumphant moment. He then went on to further his chaplaincy studies and to graduate as a prison chaplain. As a man in his seventies, his perseverance is admirable. We are proud of you, Victor!

SOMEONE WAS PRAYING
Taken from a Prayer letter

The day began with a 7 a.m. appointment — a lady, victim of satanic rites. She was quite distraught but *someone was upholding us in prayer* and she left more at peace.

When Mary arrived at 8.30a.m., we began to pray for emotional healing for traumatic events in her early childhood. All morning our mobile phones rang constantly: a girl, pleading for help with her brother affected mentally through consuming marijuana; a wife, who had just discovered that her husband has a male partner; a woman with a teenage son in deep depression; a confused man needing a listening ear and a brief prayer to set him on track.

Shortly after midday, the doorbell rang and there stood a neighbour. Her husband had given her bus fares to the hospital, to admit herself to the psychiatric ward, but her teenage daughter brought her to us instead. While Anita was praying with her, the doorbell rang again. A young man and woman, brother and sister, had arrived for their appointment after a three-hour journey. As it was their first visit, it wasn't polite to keep them waiting, so I took the 'psychiatric case' to another room and just kept on praying. She eventually came out of her trance, conversed coherently about who she is in Christ and left radiant. *Was it you who was praying at that moment?*

Meanwhile, Anita discovered that the brother and sister both had severe mental disorders. After a bit of opposition to the gospel there was a sudden breakthrough, *perhaps you were praying,* and they both received the Lord Jesus as their Saviour with tears running down their cheeks.

For some strange (?) reason, that afternoon three of our adult family arrived and decided to act like noisy teenagers. Two sources of music — from a computer and a mobile phone, caused a rather worldly atmosphere. *Was it your insistent prayer* that soon made them go back to being respectful adults?

But our day isn't over yet. It was nearly 10 p.m. when Mike and Sue arrived, all excited to show us the plans Mike was drawing up for our house extension. *Someone must have been praying,* because we were able to appear enthusiastic. Meanwhile, we were packing Joe's evening meal and flask of coffee, which I then took up the road to where he is working as night watchman. When I got back, Mike's car was still outside; the house was strangely quiet.

If someone hadn't been praying Anita wouldn't have had the ability to sit in her office and concentrate on the marriage problem they poured out into her weary ears. They left a lot happier at 20 minutes before midnight.

Anita's mobile phone woke us just after 1 a.m. For the next 10 or so minutes, I listened as she prayed with her caller, hardly pausing for breath. The caller was a pastor in deep distress. I could hear him crying loudly as he tried to fight off the spiritual attack. ***Do you sometimes wonder why you have an urge to pray for us at an unusual hour?***

HE'S NOT JUST ONE MORE PARANOID KID

The clock showed 2.05 a.m. Whoever would be banging so insistently on our front door?Only an hour had passed since we had said "goodbye" and "Happy New Year" to our guests. Woken from a deep sleep it took a while to recognise the boy from the upstairs window. Who are you? Daniel? Which Daniel? Suddenly we remembered and realised this was a serious matter. He'd come alone on a motor scooter from a town nearly two hours away. Trembling he blurted out his fear: "They are coming after me. They are going to kill me!"

After a hot drink and a time of prayer, he calmed down. We phoned his distraught parents and then put him to bed. His dad came for him next morning.

This isn't just one more 'case' of a paranoid kid. Daniel's arrival in the early hours of a new year has a special significance for us. This is the year of the Lord's favour for many prisoners, oppressed and spiritually blind people. And the news for them all is the good news: freedom won at Calvary's cross. **It's all about Him!**

NO HOPELESSLY LOST CASES

Hedrick and Annette arrived to visit us. Their radiant smiles, the tender exchange of loving looks, the hands clasped, with fingers intertwined, all spoke volumes. (No, they aren't newlyweds, they've been married for twenty years). They shared with us the miracle of Hedrick's recovery from his accident. The doctors guaranteed nothing, but God used a complicated medical situation to restore a marriage, that was practically non-existent. In the middle of the conversation, Hedrick burst out, "I guess this doesn't really have anything to do with what we're talking about, but I want to tell you, I'm so in love with my wife!"

That was a triumphant moment and equalled another triumphant moment later, when Annette burnt all the love letters and photos from her recent 'extra-marital affair'.

The reaction of most Christian people who knew their situation was, "Oh, that couple. Huh. Pretty hopeless."

We can testify that there are no 'hopelessly lost' cases in God's files.

BURSTING WITH GRATITUDE
Taken from a Prayer bulletin

It started out as a nice, normal Sunday afternoon, with our adult children coming and going, cups of coffee being shared around, just an ordinary Sunday afternoon...

– until the rain began, driven by strong gusts of wind,

– until the hail started pounding the roof, and

– until water started pouring in sheets into the living room, downstairs.

We rushed upstairs and stared transfixed at the rain pouring through the ceiling into the office. So why would we title this week's prayer bulletin, *Bursting with Gratitude?*

Simply because:

PRAISE GOD it didn't happen last weekend when we were out of town.

PRAISE GOD this weekend's retreat was cancelled, which meant we were at home at the time of the storm.

PRAISE GOD Anita felt compelled to stay in, although she had had in mind to slip out for a short time.

PRAISE GOD that John and Harvey were on hand, to carry out the heavy boxes of books and empty the cupboards.

PRAISE GOD that we have lost only about half a dozen books, out of several hundred.

PRAISE GOD that everyone who was in the house, cooperated with the enormous clean up.

PRAISE GOD that Cody climbed up on the roof, discovered the blockage and cleaned it out.

PRAISE GOD He is our loving caring Father.

No wonder we are bursting with gratitude.

ONE NEVER KNOWS
Taken from a Prayer Letter

One never knows what might occur while having breakfast

While the pastor was having breakfast with us last Monday, he received a phone call asking him to join a panel to talk about the prevention of suicide. It was just after 8 a.m. The conversation was to be recorded at 9.30 a.m. that very morning. He was a bit taken aback and asked Anita to accompany him. On Thursday afternoon we saw the programme on a local TV station. Statistics showed that suicide, unemployment and the use of anti-depressants had placed Armenia in second place for the saddest city in Colombia.

The pastor and Anita had the opportunity to give hope to the hopeless.

One never knows what one might see when drawing back the bedroom window curtains

On Saturday morning, I opened the curtains and saw the patio below strewn with broken tiles and guttering. During the night, a long piece of old, heavy guttering had broken off in the terrible storm and had crashed through the patio roof. PRAISE God for a friend who is a construction worker. He was here within a couple of hours and fixed the roof. New guttering is being made and should be in place tomorrow.

One never knows what might not happen when one turns on the tap first thing in the morning

If no water comes out, it could be it's been turned off for repair work or ... it could be, that the water meter has been stolen ... or tampered with. PRAISE God it was the latter for us, and that the meter was still sitting securely in its cement bed. The broken pipes were fixed that same morning.

One never knows if the gate will be there

Praise God for Victor. He has been working here all week making us a new gate with reinforcements. The other one, including the padlock, was sawn off its hinges by thieves, during a heavy rainstorm one night recently.

A DRUG LORD
Adapted from a Prayer Letter

What picture does the name drug lord conjure up in your mind? An overweight, well-dressed man, pockets bulging with bank notes, driving a posh car up to the entrance of his country mansion?

We met someone yesterday who completely erased that image. This man called at the house where we were making a visit. Obviously very distressed, he began sobbing as he spoke with our host. He told us that after having been free from drugs for many months, he had backslidden the previous night.

What most impacted us was not so much what he said, but the trapped-animal look in his tear-filled eyes. Here is a 47-year-old drug lord who has been involved in trafficking drugs between Colombia and Mexico. The authorities haven't caught him, but he is trapped and longing to be free.

This was our first meeting with Chuck. He grew up in a Christian family, and we found out that his father was the grocer where we bought supplies for many years. This was not a chance meeting.

Seven years' later

Come please, and form a circle of protection: **Chuck**, the drug lord who walked away from his old life, has tripped over, and is flat on his face. Now, he is so horrified and upset at his wrong doings that he has even spoken of killing himself. Gather round and shield him from the brutal attack of the enemy, who is making fun of him. Pray against feelings of guilt and worthlessness. No one is exempt from a fall. Declare God's truth over him this week. God's truth about him is more powerful than the truth of his human failure.

Some weeks further on

Prayers for Chuck are being answered. Praying through the book of Ephesians, verse by verse with him, is bringing transformation to his life.

The saga continues

Yesterday Chuck phoned in a very distressed state, speaking of throwing himself out of the window of his fifth floor apartment. That morning, he had flushed a lot of cocaine down the toilet. We got our faithful helper Nora, to pray with him over the phone until we arrived there. After half an hour of prayer, he calmed down and as we continued declaring God's Word over his life, we saw the glory of the Lord. Even his expression changed. He began to renounce many dark, evil things from his past life, which the Lord brought to his mind as we prayed.

PRAISE GOD and **don't give up praying for Chuck.** The drug world is very difficult to get out of.

Drug-lord mentality

As I write, I can hear Chuck downstairs, praying God's Word with Anita. He is back on track and moving ahead. Keep praying! The drug lord mentality **can be transformed** through the renewing of the mind.

THE DOORBELL IS RINGING
Taken from a Prayer Letter

Last week we asked you to pray for everyone who will **ring our doorbell** this month. That turns out to be quite a significant request. Read on.

When **the doorbell rang** at 11.40 a.m. on Thursday I glanced at the clock. That'll be Chuck, I thought. He's rather early.

(We'd invited Chuck, the ex-drug lord for lunch, to enjoy hearing his testimony after nine months in a rehab centre.)

It wasn't Chuck, but another ex-drug lord, Gary, visibly upset, struggling to keep his emotions under control.

Briefly, here is what he told me: He couldn't face staying in his apartment a minute longer; his wife had got herself a male friend on the social network, had moved out to live with her parents under the pretext of caring for her father; she had convinced herself they weren't married (because they didn't have a church ceremony, only one in the registry office); he had been contemplating ending his life at 'the bridge'. Then he confessed to me that he had hung a rope in his apartment. I just sat and prayed with him as he wept...

The doorbell rang again

It was Chuck. Anita took the distraught Gary away, to continue praying, while I looked at Chuck's photos of the rehab centre. A short while later, I was aware that Anita and Gary left the house together. She returned alone, bringing the rope in a plastic bag.

The sequel one year later

Gary is still alive and well. Once he understood and accepted that he must take his ex-wife down from the throne in his heart, he has carried on with life, got involved in a different church and when I met him yesterday, he told me that he's waiting to see what God has for him in the future.

INSIDE THE CLOTHES
Taken from a Prayer Letter

Tonight as we were praying the Word of God with Harvey, Romans 13:14 took on a deeper meaning. *"Clothe yourselves with the Lord Jesus Christ."* His sad eyes shone, as he grasped the truth.

When you are dressed, you are inside the clothes. God dressed Adam and Eve with skins. He put them inside them. Suddenly the enormity of Romans 8:1 crystallised in his mind: *"There is now no condemnation for those who are in Christ Jesus."*

Harvey has been in our home for a month now. His family sent him to us, a broken man, contemplating suicide. We have seen a transformation in his life through the renewing of his mind. Praying, using the actual words of Scripture has had a major part in this renewal, and the Lord is revealing Himself to Harvey. We are tremendously encouraged to see God at work in his life.

"THIS VERSE IS TALKING ABOUT ME"

Praying the Word of God with Lesley, is an exhilarating experience. As she took the words of Romans 8:15 and personalised them in prayer, the truth dawned on this young woman, for many years a slave to fears and phobias. She realised that a spirit of slavery had had her in bondage to fear.

But it was Hebrews 2:14-15 that made her literally jump to her feet. *"Since the children have flesh and blood, he too shared in their humanity so that by his death he might break the power of him who holds the power of death—that is, the devil— and free those who all their lives were held in slavery by their fear of death."*

She began to cry, as she believed the simple yet profound truth which she expressed in her own words: "This verse is talking about me! I've been in slavery for so long because I've feared death. But Jesus destroyed him who holds the power of death! I'm free from the spirit of slavery!"

Her tears turned to laughter, and we joined in and rejoiced with her.

MANY NEEDS, ONE ANSWER

We encounter many different and complex situations every day.

To mention just a few: the emotional suffering of the parents of a teenage girl who they just discover is taking drugs. This news comes on top of the anguish of discovering that her small brother has been sexually abused at his school.

We witness the devastation of a couple, who had lost a daughter and an unborn grandchild when she died suddenly.

There is May, who hears God telling her to accept the teenage girl from her husband's previous marriage, in spite of her rebellious and disruptive behaviour in the home.

A single mother, who has been saved out of a lifestyle of involvement with the occult, is asking for guidance in establishing God's Kingdom in her home.

A daughter asks us to visit and pray for peace of mind for her elderly, invalid mother, tortured by memories of an abortion...

And so it goes on.

Praise God the answer is the FINISHED work of Jesus Christ on the Cross. He has paid it all, he has forgiven all, and He is THE ANSWER!

It's all about Him.

A BRIGHT SHINING LIGHT
Adapted from a Prayer Letter

Lucero came to us in dark despair. The bitter words that spilled out of her mouth revealed her broken heart. Two broken marriages, dozens of broken relationships, she had nothing nice to say about anyone. Here is a woman who had been in Christian leadership for years. She stayed with us on two separate occasions and we witnessed a beautiful change in her outlook and reactions. God changed her from the inside, out.

A week or so after she was back home, she phoned to ask if she could bring some needy pastors to visit us. We agreed. (Pastors and leaders take priority in our ministry). Lucero, her name translates as 'morning star', had been shining. She couldn't keep quiet about the *life-changing information* that God had revealed to her. She told us she had a long list of people in leadership that need to restore their relationship with God, and that she was going to bring them one by one. So, because of Lucero's testimony, Vera stayed for a week and her husband came the following week. Keep shining Lucero!

P.S. Lucero is now with the Lord.

GLASS OBJECTS AND WEIRD BEADS

"I've been going to church for seven years and no one ever told me I should get rid of all these things."

Laura, a wealthy lawyer, asked us to visit her home and help her to make decisions. She had begun the task early that morning and had a heap of things on the spare bed.

We gaze at the pile. Once a devout catholic, she has an enormous assortment of images, angels, virgins, crucifixes, all costly, some even from Rome itself. There are several little bottles of holy water, a candle burnt at her mother's wake, but wait… what is all this other stuff?

Piles of ornate mirrors, glass objects, weird beads. This is New Age stuff, and still Laura keeps bringing more and more things: grotesque objects that are Halloween decorations, books written by gurus, catholic prayers, oh, and this: she hands over a plastic bag.

"This is the rope." She pauses and looks up at the beams on the bedroom ceiling: "I was going to do it up there."

SOUNDS PRETTY DESPERATE

"I'm playing my last card."

Judy announced her desperate decision. Her husband, a pastor, was at his wits end; her ministry, her physical and emotional state, not to mention her marriage and her children, were suffering.

Judy travelled seven hours over the Andes Mountains and stayed in our home for three weeks.

She submitted to the Lord and permitted Him to thoroughly spring-clean her life. When she forgave those who had wronged her, her facial expression changed; when she allowed the Lord to heal a long-time bitter memory, the tight painful knot in her stomach, vanished. She was free to laugh and to sing. (She sang herself hoarse, while standing on the back of a jeep, on one of our outings into the countryside.)

*** *** ***

"I've swallowed my front teeth."

James mumbled his desperate situation. His bridge, with its three teeth, was stuck half way down his oesophagus.

Several hours later, I prayed with him as he lay on a stretcher waiting to be operated on. Suddenly the doctor decided to have him transferred to another hospital. The desperate situation forged a link with the family.

And the teeth?

The bridge made its way slowly on down James' digestive tract and found its way out all by itself.

DEEP WATERS
Taken from a Prayer Letter

I have before me a newspaper cutting, and read the horrifying statistics of the suicide rate among children and young people in Colombia.

Today, I don't write about statistics, but about a family tragedy.

Elsie was one of our daycare children 20 years ago. Last week at the age of 21 she hung herself with a rope in her parents' kitchen.

What happened? At what point did she begin to listen to Satan's voice? Quite some time ago it seems. Her father recalls the day six months ago, when she bought a rope.

The source of the voice? Her computer stored the death-provoking subliminal messages of heavy metal music. Her friends appeared at the funeral, Satanists dressed in black, who commented that it was "her turn" and wondered who was next.

We weep with her parents who are passing through deep waters where the questions have no answers.

We minister comfort to the broken hearted family and gently guide them to the only One who can fill their aching void.

BLACK WATERS

The Lord impressed upon us to travel half an hour to a nearby village to pray with Elsie's bereaved parents, every day for seven days. These concentrated prayer vigils always come under direct attack from the enemy. Last week was no exception.

On the second day, a neighbour came to our door to tell us that a dark brown liquid was seeping from a crack in the pavement outside our house. The smell confirmed our suspicion: 'black waters', the Spanish words for sewerage. For the following three days, while the cracked pipe was dug up and replaced, not one tap could be used in our house. Quite a complicated situation, but we survived. Meals were made in one place, showers taken in another. We refused to let the 'black waters' deter our prayer vigils with Elsie's parents.

CHASED BY AN ANGEL

When our phone rang shortly before 3.00 a.m., it was bad news. A woman, pretending to be a home visitor from the Child Welfare department had snatched Don's two small children from their mother. The 22-month-old girl was found within hours, after a woman reported that she'd found her abandoned on a street corner. Baby Jeff was still missing. The story hit national newspapers and TV. Hastily, we alerted praying people around the world. One person prayed Psalm 35:5 very specifically: *"Let the angel of the Lord chase them."*

Two days later, across the other side of town, an agitated woman with a baby in her arms, knocked on a door. She asked to use the phone. When told there wasn't a phone in the house, she suddenly handed over the baby.

"Hold him for a moment, while I look for a public phone," she said, as she hurried away.

The police were called and Baby Jeff was identified and reunited with his family. We prayed with them for emotional healing.

The woman never came back. Most likely she's still running…

UNEXPECTED ANSWER

I am convinced that praying for our streets and local community is on God's agenda, so I invited the Christians who live in our immediate neighbourhood to a weekly prayer time in our home. We prayed for our local shopkeepers, the local school staff and pupils, as well as for the particular situations we face as a community, e.g. a group of Satanists who gather in the next block, the kids who smoke marijuana on the basketball court across the road.

One answer to our prayers was totally unexpected. Among those we were praying for, was the owner and staff of a small grocery store. We started praying for them by name.

Imagine our horror one night, to hear machine-gun fire. Two

of the grocery store staff had been gunned down right there on the premises. Stunned, we joined the enormous crowd that immediately gathered. I hugged the owner and let her cry on my shoulder. Her son lay dead on the ground barely three metres from where we stood. Scary questions hung in the chilly night air. Why this horrific violence in our neighbourhood? Were we not praying for these very people?

The unexpected answer came quietly into my heart at about 4 a.m. next morning.

"I am answering your prayers for a clean neighbourhood."

The truth soon surfaced. These people were involved in the mafia and sold heroin under the counter.

"Thank You Lord. You are cleaning up our community."

And the sequel? The new grocery store owners are Christians.

NEW CREATURES DO NEW THINGS

Matt and Amelia, a church-going couple, were soundly converted at one of our Broken Cisterns seminars. They became new creatures in Christ, and decided they wanted to get married as born-again Christians. They emphasised it wasn't just to renew vows, but to get married as new creatures in Christ. That caused quite a stir in their church. Were they not already married?

Their sincerity in cleaning up their lives before the big date was amazing. They suspended life as a married couple, came for spiritual help separately, and were willing to free themselves from all that bound them to the aggressive life-style they had become accustomed to living. There was much to forgive, much to learn about godly roles in marriage. They persevered. The romance blossomed before the wondering eyes of his son, her son and their son.

The ceremony was unique. The bride walked up the aisle between the two teenage sons, and the six-year-old carried the rings. When the moment came to make their vows, Matt looked up to Heaven and spoke to God Himself. He made his vows to God, not to his wife.

He understood that faithfulness in the marriage is to God. **It's all about Him.**

I'VE NEVER FORGOTTEN

"Anita-Katalina!"

We both looked over to where the voice came from. A man was getting off his motorcycle. He removed his helmet and came over to us. Grinning broadly, he looked from one to the other quizzically.

"Which is Anita, which is Katalina?"

We introduced ourselves, as he continued.

"I'll never forget what you taught us – the Wordless Book, there was a red page and a gold page and a white page. I was in your Bible class and you gave us leaflets. I saved them all."

In a flash, we were back in the room packed with children. In the front row, a little boy with a broad grin drank in every word of our beginner's Spanish.

"That was thirty six years ago."

"Yes, it was thirty six years ago, but I've never forgotten."

As we parted, we reminded him that more important than keeping all the leaflets we had handed out, was to have Jesus Christ in his heart.

Apart from Lucero, all names have been changed.

*** *** ***

Seeing God work in the lives of so many, takes our breath away. It's harvest time and we are kept running with baskets to catch the fruit! His Word is so powerful and He is changing lives radically. **It's all about Him.**

REAL LIFE

The LORD is good, a refuge in times of trouble.
He cares for those who trust in him.

Nahum 1:7

AN EXPERIENCE THAT DEFIES DESCRIPTION

It's a normal Monday afternoon. Twenty-one people have enjoyed lunch at our place. Suddenly, with an ominous growl, the house shudders, and then jerks violently. Some scramble for shelter under the big oak dining table. Nell* clings to a doorpost that rocks to and fro. Victor sits paralysed in an armchair. Part of the ceiling crashes on to the table as roof and rafters fall in. Time stands still, as our world collapses. Armenia, the city we know and love, disappears forever — in 19 seconds, January 25, 1999.

No words

No words can adequately describe an experience that defies description.

There are no words – Only the gasping sobs of Maria, who watches as a wall crushes her daughter. Only a sickening thud, as a block of concrete knocks the life from a pretty teenage girl. No words can describe the terror in the eyes of the passengers, as a deluge of red bricks rains over a bus. Their hands stretch out the windows in a futile attempt to grasp at life. A thousand thousand tiles crash to the ground. Wood groans and splinters. Lengths of iron twist grotesquely around the bodies of three children. Skulls grin from graves wrenched open. Cars crumple beyond recognition. Walls fall out and flatten pedestrians. Walls fall in and trap whole families. Nearly 36 thousand homes are destroyed — in 19 seconds.

There are no words – Only wild distorted thoughts and frantic questions. *The end of the world? The beast? Where are my children? Is this what it feels like to die?* Can words convey the confusion, the chaos? All the fire engines lie crumpled beneath tonnes of concrete. The police scrabble to rescue members of their force, buried under the ruins of their headquarters. The unhappy wailing of ambulance sirens fills the air. There are no words. Only the cacophony of human voices: the living shout; the wounded scream; the dying moan. Pandemonium breaks loose as the able, carrying the wounded, flag down taxis. Rubble blocks the streets. Red dust from countless broken bricks chokes the air. Rain starts falling. People run. They search wildly for familiar faces, for family. Some wander like zombies. A thoughtful stranger takes Ana's arm and guides her across the road. Kneeling in the street, Alf raises his arms heavenwards and shouts his thanks to God for saving his family. People run without direction, in the pouring rain.

There are no words – Only frantic digging. With super-human strength, rescuers heave concrete blocks aside. Outside the cake shop, grim faced helpers lay 19 bodies along the pavement. No words can measure the joy surging inside Matilde, as she wriggles from the rubble with her living granddaughter. Sitting down on a chunk of cement, she tenderly picks the plaster out of her hair and wipes the dust off her tiny face. Can mere words register the pain a four-year-old suffers with a broken pelvis? Or the agony in the heart of the father stumbling across the city with the limp body of his nine-year-old daughter in his arms? Can words record the pain level of the hundreds wounded and waiting under the rubble? Or the agony of soul of those who stand and stare at the mountains of debris covering their loved ones?

Tears

There just aren't any words. Only tears.

Tears for Carl who drags his father from the ruins of their home, and finds his legs are partially severed.

Tears for this valiant man, who squeezes his son's hand and tells him good-bye.

Tears for Stephanie, my seven-year-old Sunday School pupil, crushed to death by bricks and mortar.

No words, only tears, for the widow under a sheet of plastic, keeping vigil alone, by a coffin.

Tears for the bewildered old man, slumped in a plastic chair in the middle of a deserted street.

There are no words, only hot scalding tears for the stark fear in Jim's eyes, as he tells us how, alone, he defended his family home from looters.

Fear freezes the tears on our cheeks, a fear stronger than sorrow.

Fear

The pounding of our hearts competes with the pounding feet of the looters. We lock our door and fear for our neighbours, who have no door to lock. Volunteers arm themselves with knives and sticks. And courage. They organise vigils, burn rubber tyres, protect their wives and children. And us. The sound of gunfire converts our dreams to nightmares. We long for daylight.

There are no words to describe the awful fear that engulfs the little girls thrown to the ground, beaten and raped by the looters; indescribable fear in the heart of the once-prosperous businessperson, as paralysed, he watches looters carry off his merchandise.

Loss

There are no words to calculate the losses.

Ninety per cent of the city-centre collapses. Henry, the TV technician loses his son and his workshop at the same moment. He is still dazed, when I phone him three weeks later.

Olympica Supermarket is looted. Splinters of glass litter the floor. Fruit and vegetables pounded to pulp, rot in the aisles. The shelves are empty.

Yesterday the open market place thronged with people. Today, only a stray dog sniffs among the stalls smashed to matchsticks. Livelihoods are lost.

Numb with grief, bowed figures move slowly through the makeshift morgues, searching for lost loved ones.

Rosa is one of many children who lose their world. The back-street alley with its sweet and sour atmosphere has gone. She has no home, no toys, and no corner shop. No father.

When 95% of Brasilia is obliterated from the map, Jim loses his suburb. An orange and white painted door is all that identifies his home among the debris. I feel sad as I watch children fossick among his family's belongings. Nothing is sacred anymore.

The homeless lose their privacy. Blue and green painted portable toilets stand in full view of passing traffic. Temporary showers are rigged up behind sheets of tin. A harassed mother tries to shelter her children from the unsavoury comments of lewd men. Lines of washing stretch along the main road. A spotty faced youth scrubs the cuff of his grubby jacket just centimetres from a passing bus, while a man holding a broken piece of mirror, balances on a heap of rubble and shaves his chin. Privacy is a lost luxury. The city loses her dignity, her pride, her landmarks, and her identity.

Bereavement

Our whole city is grieving, mourning for losses both collective and personal.

We are all bereaved. Our behaviour is bizarre, out of character, the behaviour of the bereaved.

Some days we sit and look at the mess, with no inclination to clean up. We dress in jeans and old t-shirts. For weeks, we lie down at night fully dressed. We feel irritable for no reason, jump at sudden noises. Many complain of headaches. Clara suffers from fainting spells. Middle-aged Sue sleeps on the sofa, in a track suit and running shoes. There is only one topic of conversation — the earthquake.

Frustration

Frustration is at its highest level.

We have no phones, no banks, no post office, and no shops. Nowhere to buy plastic sheeting to cover the gaping hole, where the roof fell in. It rains every day, and we run out of buckets to catch the rain pouring through to the ground floor. As fast as we put the cats out the back door, they climb in through the open roof and disturb our nights with their boisterous games. The very pettiness of the frustrations makes them all the more frustrating. For over a week, no buses run. When they start again, all the routes have been changed. We feel like we are in a strange city.

Admiration

In this strange city, everyone begins again.

The homeless have not lost their creativity, their ingenuity. Every conceivable type of accommodation springs up in the most unlikely places: under the trees in the middle of an avenue, in a vacant lot, in parks, in children's playgrounds. Bamboo poles and plastic sheeting are the most popular materials. The architecture is original.

The ingenuity of the people is admirable. Overnight, they hook up cables to the power poles. TV sets blare. Fans whir. They link their salvaged telephones to the phone lines, and converse comfortably in their plastic shelters. They tap into the main water pipes and boast of running water. A car wheel rim makes an excellent stove top, and there's plenty of wood for the fire underneath. I feel privileged to be entertained in these homes of the homeless. The majority are optimistic and grateful to be alive.

Gratitude

"Thank God I'm alive," is the phrase on everyone's lips.

I look at the twisted remains of my bed and agree. There are no words to express our profound gratitude to God for all His goodness. Gratitude for the missionaries and Colombians from other cities who bring us sheets of plastic, food and water and cash; for those who stop by, just to hug us; for those who phone us long distance and let us talk as long as we need; for Harry, the rag-bag bottle and bone man who keeps our spirits up the first night, when everyone sleeps in the street; for the angels God sends to protect us; for a sense of humour that diffuses tense situations; for Claude, the civil engineer, who offers to oversee all reconstruction work; for protection from injury, when he falls through the roof; for deepened friendships with neighbours; for opportunities to preach the gospel; and for the prayers of Christians worldwide. There are no words that adequately express our gratitude. We can only re-dedicate our lives to God because He has given us life.

All names have been changed to protect the identity of our Colombian family and friends.

WICKED AND FRUSTRATED

An international flight of 17 hours, coupled with a bag-snatching incident in the airport, on our arrival back in Colombia, had left us tense, without personal identification and practically broke. Home was still another 35 minutes flight away. Eagerly I dialled our home telephone number to inform our house caretaker of our arrival time next day.

The voice that answered the phone was not the voice I expected. My mind raced dizzily from one possible clue to another, as I demanded an explanation. What was George* from our church, doing in our house at 11 o'clock at night?

I couldn't get any satisfactory information out of either George, or the caretaker. From what I could gather, the latter had a nasty fright and got in touch with Mario, the pastor, who had sent George to keep him company. I immediately phoned Mario. He presented me with the cold facts: attempted robbery.

I replaced the receiver and realised I was trembling. At my side, my sister had heard the frightening news. Our eyes locked in a horrified stare.

Upstairs in bed we rehearsed every detail of my phone conversation. I seriously doubted if I'd understood what I'd just heard. So did my sister.

Suddenly she asked: "What was the last part of our special verse?" Then added, "Look it up."

I started at her question. Our verse! I flicked on the light and pulled my Bible towards me, feeling a thrill of excitement as my eyes scanned Psalm 146:9. I read aloud: *"The Lord watches over the alien and sustains the fatherless and the widow, but frustrates the ways of the wicked."*

Wow! That last phrase threw light on the mystery. Somewhere, someone must be feeling very frustrated.

I switched off the lamp and relaxed. My mind went back to when, before our visit to New Zealand, I'd read that verse in my devotional reading. It had given us confidence as we left Colombia. I liked the feeling of comfort it gave me now.

I savoured the first phrase: *"The Lord looks after the alien."* That was quite obvious from our experience in the airport on arrival. I went through the details one by one.

In the bag snatched off our luggage trolley was my passport, my Colombian ID card, bank card and the American dollars we'd needed to change into pesos on arrival. After I'd reported the theft to the police, I'd phoned our bank to freeze the account. I'd been perturbed when they told me how much money we had, because we had been relying on a fairly large sum having been paid in during our time away.

I sighed as I thought about my lost wallet. Without cash, we'd had to change our plans. How we'd longed for a couple of days on our own, to recover from jet-lag. Instead, we'd reluctantly phoned a friend to put us up. I felt the prickle of tears behind my eyes as I recalled her reaction and her words on hearing about our stolen bag.

"About that money I owe you. I didn't get round to putting it in your account. I've got the cash here in the house."

She'd handed it to us in a new wallet. It covered our plane ticket for the last lap of our journey.

The second part of the verse had come true too. *"He sustains the fatherless and the widow."* All our 15 Colombian children had been satisfactorily placed before we'd left the country. Even the mentally handicapped boy and our homeless cook had been looked after.

I opened my eyes and stared into the darkness, trying to make sense out of what Mario had just told me.

Who was this wicked woman who had been frustrated in her plans? She'd tricked the caretaker into believing we'd given orders for several items of furniture to be taken away. Was it really true that our enormous fridge had been on the footpath, ready to be lifted on to a jeep? I wondered which neighbour had intervened. Everything had been taken back into the house, Mario then informed me.

I was totally confused and rather scared. But as I lay there thinking, one thing was clear: God was obviously in charge of the situation. A promise was a promise. *"He frustrates the ways of the wicked"* (Psalm 146:9).

I decided I'd trust Him with what I didn't understand. I turned over and fell asleep.

The air was tense as we walked into our home the following afternoon. I glanced around nervously. Everything was in place.

It took several days to sift through the information that the embarrassed caretaker gave us, and to interview the neighbours. Everyone wanted to hear all the details, and so they all got to hear about our special Scripture verse. Each time we told our story, we had the opportunity to give God the glory; each time we did so, our faith in Him grew stronger.

Life settled down and other things claimed our attention, but always in the background there were the disturbing questions that had no answers. Who was she? What was she after? Had she taken anything?

The answer arrived in the mail nearly two months later: our USA bank statement. It showed that two cheques had been presented during our time out of Colombia. I tingled all over as I pulled them out of the envelope.

They were written out to a woman. I gasped audibly. The name fitted all the descriptions of our intruder. She'd forged the cheques with a combination of our signatures and signed her name on the reverse side, along with her ID number and her parents' phone number.

How frustrated she would be when she realised how much evidence she'd helped us with.

But then, God frustrates the ways of the wicked, doesn't He?

*All names have been changed

CLOTHES FOR THE NAKED AND OTHER SITUATIONS

"I have given them the glory that you gave me,
that they may be one as we are one."
John 17:22

CLOTHES FOR THE NAKED

"Yer naked."

The man pointed an accusing finger at the woman in front of him.

"Speak for yerself," she replied, her mouth twisted in contempt.

Mesmerised, they stared at one another.

Suddenly, something akin to an electric shock, passed through their naked bodies, leaving them weak. They both began to shake uncontrollably.

There were no words in their vocabulary to express what they were feeling. Vulnerable, ashamed and yes, totally naked. Something was missing.

Their eyes met and both recognised in the eyes of the other, something they were unable to explain.

Fear. Shame. We have the appropriate vocabulary. They didn't.

Lost. Destitute.

Destitute of the Glory of God, those beautiful clothes God had dressed them in, were gone.

Up until that moment, they had seen one another covered with the Glory of God. They had never seen nakedness.

In a futile intent to cover themselves, they grabbed some leaves.

Fig leaves. It wasn't a sensible choice as they were soon to discover. Although the size was in their favour, the texture certainly was not. The rough, prickly surface was extremely uncomfortable.

The woman screwed up her face in pain and her eyes filled with tears.

*** *** ***

Is there hope for the human race, which, since that tragic day, has been born spiritually naked and destitute of the Glory of God?

Are there clothes to cover that nakedness?

Is it possible that we could leave off seeing the nakedness of our fellow men and begin to see one another in the light of the Glory of God?

*** *** ***

Come with me, and listen to a conversation between a son and his father.

"... *Father, just as you are in me and I am in you. May they also be in us so that the world may believe that you have sent me. I have given them the glory that you gave me, that they may be one as we are one: I in them and you in me...*" (John 17:21-23).

This conversation between the Son, Jesus and His Father, God, gives answers to the questions we have just asked. We can get back the clothing which Adam and Eve wore — the Glory of God.

If I am clothed with the Glory of God, I will not see the nakedness of my brother. I will see him in the light of the Glory of God; I will see him dressed with the Glory of God.

*** *** ***

"Not again. I just can't believe it."

Dazed, the woman puts her mobile phone on the table and flops into the armchair. Certain scenes from a film start running through her head, the earlier ones equally clear as the more recent.

She sees as if it were yesterday, her husband in the pulpit, in front of a large congregation. Everyone is clapping.

She hears the youth group shouting with approval when he is named their leader, but somehow today the congratulations sound hollow and mocking; the applause reverberates like stones hitting against a wall.

She sees the country folk from a farming community begging him to teach them from the Bible. Someone shouts, "We will study the Bible as long as Orlando* is our teacher."

She hears the giggles from the girls sitting on the front row of the church building. They never miss a service. Orlando is their hero.

Then she remembers when he began to counsel a certain young lady. She sought him out, she continually phoned him, she pressured him, and… she seduced him.

The woman shudders as she relives those moments of betrayal. She clenches her fists in anger.

"Good for nothing minx."

She frowns and wonders whether her husband has really repented. She asks herself a question. *Has the effort she made to walk alongside him in the thorny restoration process, been worth it?*

For a long time she sits and thinks about what she learnt during the entire sordid situation.

Her mobile phone ring-tone startles her. She listens as another woman spews out the latest gossip. Again. Deep inside she knows it isn't gossip. It's adultery. Again.

*** *** ***

Kneeling by the old armchair, the broken young woman asks herself repeatedly how she should react. She begins to pray.

Hours pass. When she rises from her knees she knows what she must do, how she should react. She takes a crumpled, stained sheet of paper from her bedside table and begins to read aloud.

"Thank You Lord for giving Orlando the right to be Your child. I confess that he is a child of God because he has received You and has believed in Your name" (John 1:12).

"Lord, Orlando's body is Your temple because the Holy Spirit lives in him. You bought him with the highest price in the universe – Your precious blood. Teach him to honour You with his body" (1 Corinthians 8:19, 20).

The young wife takes a deep breath in an effort to fight off the thoughts that pour into her mind. Undesirable scenes dance in front of her eyes but she decides to believe who her husband is, in Christ. She carries on reading.

"Thank You Lord for rescuing Orlando from the dominion of darkness. I declare that Satan has no power over him. He belongs to the kingdom of Jesus Christ forever" (Colossians 1:13).

"Thank You, Lord, that You came to destroy the works of the devil. I proclaim that all the works of the devil in Orlando's life are destroyed" (1 John 3:8).

"Thank You, Lord, that you chose Orlando before the creation of the world to be holy and blameless in Your sight. Thank You that it is Your blood that makes him holy. I declare that Orlando is holy" (Ephesians 1:4).

Holy? He is holy after what he has done? The words shout in her mind. She gasps as she recognises the source: it is human truth trying to assert itself against God's truth. She shouts back: "In Christ, Orlando is holy. I believe what God says about him. The blood of Jesus makes him holy!"

She shudders at her own audacity. Beads of cold sweat appear on her forehead. She reaches for a paper handkerchief, wipes her face and then with an effort, returns to the sheet of paper.

"Thank You, God, for forgiving all Orlando's sins and for cancelling the written code that was against him" (Colossians 2:13, 14). "You have justified him and there is nobody who can condemn him" (Romans 8:33).

"Lord I declare that Orlando has been given the victory through the Lord Jesus Christ" (1 Corinthians 15:57). "He is more than a conqueror" (Romans 8:37).

*** *** ***

Every morning before daybreak, this valiant woman wakes up to declare God's truth about the man sleeping at her side. She doesn't deny human truth; she simply decides that it will not distract her from her decision to believe who her husband is in Christ. She decides to clothe him with the Glory of God in order not to look at his nakedness. She sees him dressed with the Glory of God. She sees him in Christ.

The days go by. As she prepares the meals in her kitchen, this determined young lady wields her powerful spiritual weapons. Firmly, she repeats who her husband is in Christ: "Orlando is redeemed; he is justified, washed in the blood of the Lord Jesus. Orlando is sanctified; he is a new creature in Christ. He is complete in Christ. Orlando has the mind of Christ. I decide to believe who he is in Christ."

*** *** ***

You ask me, how did it all end?

This is a true story.

The day came when Orlando voluntarily confessed his sin and was restored, simply because his wife decided to put on one side the weapons of the flesh — her anger, her disappointment, her desire for vengeance, even her emotional pain. She chose to cover his nakedness and see her husband in Christ. She chose the best covering — she clothed him with Christ.

Not his real name.

GOODBYE ANXIETY

"Humble yourselves, therefore, under God's mighty hand, that he may lift you up in due time. Cast all your anxiety on him because he cares for you" (1 Peter 5:6-7).

We like verse 7, but if we are totally honest we aren't too keen on the first phrase of v 6! It goes against the grain to humble ourselves. Perhaps we shy away from that mighty hand because it brings us memories of what we were taught and we still have that picture of an angry God waiting to bring His hand down hard on his wayward child. If that is the case, who wouldn't want to get away from the mighty hand? But these two verses are related. So much so, that we can't cast our cares on Him unless we are actually under the mighty hand!

When the Israelites were under the cloud, they were safe. They were protected. The mighty hand is a protecting hand. It is where we are totally safe. It is where we know we are loved. There we depend on Him and trust His wisdom, His counsel. It is a place of complete security. So, who wouldn't choose to be there!

In that secure place, under the mighty hand, we are in a position to cast our cares and anxiety on Him, because it is there, that we believe that He really does care for us!

So, first things first: "Lord, I renounce my own will and choose to depend on You in this situation, in this decision. I believe You have my best interests at heart. I rely on You. I choose to submit my will to Yours. I renounce worry and accept that it is pride, where in effect I am saying that You are not capable enough to deal with my problem. I choose to humble myself under Your mighty hand. I trust the protecting power of that hand."

Then: "I hand my anxiety to You Lord. I confess that my anxiety is an affront to Your care for me. I trust You with this situation, this person, this problem. I relax under Your mighty hand and enjoy the protection it gives me. Thank You Father."

LIFE-CHANGING INFORMATION

"Perhaps today."

Anna's pulse quickened as she whispered the words. She rose stiffly from the stone floor, where she had been kneeling. Her spirit stirred deep down inside her. She'd felt a similar stirring many years earlier, on the eve of her wedding day.

"The same, yet somehow different," she mused, as she rubbed her sore knees.

"I'm expecting something exciting," she decided.

Slowly she made her way across the Temple courtyard towards a couple with a baby.

Suddenly Anna knew.

"Praise God! Hallelujah!"

She raised her withered arms. Tears rained down her crinkly cheeks.

"The Messiah has come…"

Oblivious of the startled onlookers, Anna looked up to Heaven and spoke directly to God.

The bewildered mother hugged her baby and stared at the little old woman.

"The baby… the Messiah… the promise fulfilled."

The girl savoured the words and stored them away in her heart.

***

"Humph. That old woman drives me up the wall. Every day the same story about the same baby."

The rabbi flicked a tiresome gnat from his wide sleeve. He shifted uneasily on the stone bench. Change was in the wind and he felt uncomfortable.

He knew, because all who studied the law knew, that one day the Messiah would come. But he didn't like what he was hearing too many times a day, every day. Surely, God wouldn't trust a woman with such life-changing information.

He stiffened.

There she is again. Same story. Same baby.

Through narrowed eyes, he watched Anna hobble over to a group of newcomers to the Temple. Her wrinkled face was radiant. Grudgingly the rabbi admitted that her toothless smile was, well almost, beautiful. Her words floated across the courtyard.

"Baby... Messiah... promise fulfilled."

The rabbi resolutely closed his ears.

*** *** ***

"Come and see a man who knew all about the things I did, who knows me inside and out."

The woman paused for breath and then continued, "Do you think this could be the Messiah?"

Heads swivelled. Necks craned forward. Eyebrows shot up.

Opinions circled the village within minutes.

The woman wiped the perspiration from her forehead. In the middle of the open market place, they closed in on her, elbowing their way to her side, demanding details.

"Come and see," she repeated.

The woman's testimony was enough to convince them. The Messiah had arrived. Excitedly they pushed and shoved one another towards Jacob's well.

He talked to them. They listened. Information became revelation. They believed.

The shadows lengthened, yet still they lingered, listening and believing.

"Come and stay with us," they begged.

Enthusiastically the crowd headed back to the village with the Jew who not only talked to them, but also accepted the invitation to stay in their village.

They hung on His words. They asked questions. They believed.

They said to the woman, "We've heard it for ourselves and know it for sure. He's the Saviour of the world."

Life-changing information.

*** *** ***

"He's gone."

Mary shifted the bundle of spices she carried, to relieve the ache in her arms. The ache in her heart intensified.

She had no tears left to weep, just a dull constant pain behind her eyes. With every step she took towards the tomb of her loved one, the words throbbed in her temples: *gone, dead and buried.*

Preparing the spices had taken longer than she had imagined, but when she had lain down, sleep had evaded her. Dejected and utterly weary, she felt as if every vestige of hope had been sucked from her soul.

She wasn't on her own. Other women walked alongside her, but she walked in the aloneness of the bereaved.

***

"He's gone."

Mary gasped. The enormous stone was not in the cave opening. She pushed in front of the others, to see inside for herself. It was dark. When her eyes adjusted to the interior, she saw it was true. There was no body.

The women's eyes locked in a terrified stare, and then puzzled, they stood gazing into the emptiness.

Suddenly two men, in clothes that shone with the intensity of lightning, dazzled the mourners. They appeared from nowhere. Terror-stricken, the women hid their faces and bowed down.

One of the men spoke to them. What they heard was life-changing information.

"Why are you looking for a living person here? This is a place for the

dead. Jesus is not here. He has risen from death! Do you remember what he said in Galilee? He said that the Son of Man must be given to evil men, be killed on a cross, and rise from death on the third day" (Luke 24:5-7 ICB).

As a movie rewound in slow motion, the conversation came back to Mary's befuddled mind. Of course, she hadn't understood at the time, but she did remember. Now she believed.

There was only one thing to do. She had life-changing information that couldn't wait.

All tiredness vanished. With the other women chasing behind her, Mary lifted up her skirts and ran.

***

The group of excited women burst into the room, all talking at once. The words flew from their open mouths like birds escaping from a cage.

"Not there!"

"Risen!"

"Alive!"

The men's reaction abruptly silenced their twittering.

"Stuff and nonsense." Thomas rolled his eyes.

"Female fantasy." James suppressed a snigger.

"Tell us another. Would a woman be trusted with such information?" Andrew scoffed.

"OK. We'll see." Peter left the room.

Mary heaved a sigh. The emotional impact was taking its toll. However, of one thing she was sure: her life had changed forever.

MY OWN PSALM

An ominous clunk silenced our singing and laughter. With a tremendous shudder, the bus halted. Amid stifled shrieks and an entwined mass of sunburnt arms and legs, we threw ourselves off the panting vehicle.

Three weeks later, I sat with the organisers of that bus trip, composing a psalm of gratitude to God for His goodness to us during our women's national retreat. Our visitors had gone back to their homes all over Colombia. We, the host church, gathered to evaluate our accomplishment.

Suddenly, the full impact of that dangerous situation hit us. Had the axle broken on a curve or as we sped along the open road, our outing would have ended in tragedy. More than one caught her breath, as I wrote on the board: "We prayed for protection on our outing and He saved us from tragedy, because God is merciful. We proved this during our retreat."

As we enumerated blessing after blessing, the psalm - our psalm - unfolded before our eyes. We saw God's goodness, His mercy, His greatness, His faithfulness. Our hearts burst with gratitude. Praise and adoration poured from our lips.

Together, we discovered that to reflect on the attributes of God, cultivates an attitude of praise and thanksgiving. Together, we composed the psalm, our own song of praise, entitled Psalm 151.

We based our psalm on the format of Psalm 136. It opens with this magnificent statement: HE IS GOOD.

It's easy to believe that God is good when an accident has been avoided or a patient makes a miraculous recovery. Is He still good when the accident occurs or the patient dies? The question of suffering pounds at the door and demands an answer. Satan hisses at our heels: "Is God really good?" Tiny doubts nibble at our Sunday School faith.

Verses 2 and 3 of Psalm 136 exalt Him as the God of gods and the Lord of lords: Omnipotent, omniscient, omnipresent.

My class of seven and eight-year-olds twist their tongues around those grand words, as they would round a sticky caramel. Why do I teach them these abstract ideas?

Jill Briscoe, in her book, *Running on Empty*, gives the answer. I quote: "We need to 'learn' God in the days before the night comes – to learn what He looks like, and what He acts like, and what He says."

What we learned in Sunday School is true. God IS good.

In 1996, I went home from the mission field to care for my mother who was terminally ill. Time lay heavily on my hands during the bleak winter months. More to occupy myself than anything else, I bought an exercise book and at the top of each page, I wrote an attribute of God. Then I began reading through the Psalms. I noted every mention of His holiness, His power, His mercy, His goodness. I never finished, because my mother died early in the spring, but through that simple exercise I 'learned' God. The refresher course prepared me to accept her death. God Himself hugged me, as I grieved.

"His love endures forever" (Psalm 136:1).

Herbert vander Lugt, a contributor to *Our Daily Bread* devotional readings, tells us that during a television interview, David Frost asked former President George Bush, how he could square his belief in a loving and all-powerful God with the miseries and injustices of life. Frost reminded Bush of the time he'd shed tears at the sight of starving children, and of his grief when his own daughter died.

President Bush said, "It never occurred to me to blame God for that." He insisted that the Lord had provided enough food for everyone, but that starvation occurs because of human greed and ineptitude. The President said that his daughter's illness had drawn the family closer to one another and to God. He was comforted, because he knew that she had been caught up in the arms of her loving heavenly Father.

"His love endures forever." This triumphant refrain enables us to wipe our eyes and worship Him.

The Psalmist then presents God as the Creator (Psalm 136:4-7). Acknowledge Him, as the Creator and we will never run short of reasons to thank and praise Him.

No one put it more succinctly than David did in Psalm 8:3. *"When I consider your heavens, the work of your fingers, the moon and the stars which you have set in place, what is man that you are mindful of him or the son of man that you care for him?"*

Franklin D. Roosevelt used to have a curious ritual with his friend and naturalist William Beebe. After dinner, they would go outside and look up into the night sky. They would find the lower left-hand corner of the great square of Pegasus. One of them would then recite these words: "That is the spiral galaxy of Andromeda. It is as large as our Milky Way. It is one of a hundred million galaxies. It is 750,000 light years away. It consists of a hundred billion suns, each one larger than our sun." Then they would pause for a few moments, and Roosevelt would finally say, "Now I think we feel small enough! Let's go to bed."

Did Psalm 8:3 come to Roosevelt's mind? A long look up into the night sky stimulates my worship, too.

When I use Psalm 136 as the pattern for my personal psalm, I exalt God as all-caring (verses 16-25). Not necessarily lifting us out of difficult circumstances but caring for us and supporting us in them. Three clear-cut examples of difficult circumstances, stand out:

Verse 16: *"To Him who led His people through the desert."*

The desert? So there is a desert? An inescapable, dry, dusty experience that stretches into weeks, months or even years?

A missionary friend told me about his desert experience. The project, which he had come to head up in Colombia, crumbled into dust. He received no satisfaction from a task accomplished; no prospect of future involvement. No clearly marked roads; no signpost appeared to direct him. God Himself led him through, one step at a time.

Verse 23: *"... to the One who remembered us in our low estate."*

So there could be a low estate? It's OK to let slip that I'm down?

As my sister and I walked through the glass doors with the sign 'Passengers Only' I looked back at my recently widowed father. He stood a little apart from the rest of the group. What was he thinking as we left him to return to the mission field? Three weeks later, he told us in a letter.

He wrote, "Thank you for your lovely hugs. I felt so joyful to see you go where the Lord would have you be. Whatever the Lord has in the future for us – it's His **good** and **perfect** will."

I am comforted to realise, that even while our eyes are full of tears, our hearts can be full of praise and thanksgiving. Because He understands and remembers me.

In his book, *God Came Near,* Max Lucado reassures me that "the challenge to leave family for the gospel was issued by the One who kissed His mother goodbye in the doorway."

Verse 24 gives the third example of adverse circumstances: *"... and freed us from our enemies."*

Enemies? Well, yes. The armour God gives us in Ephesians chapter 6 is to protect us from our enemies. There are plenty around. Phil Phillips exposes the occult connection in toys marketed to unsuspecting children. His book, *Turmoil in the Toybox,* arms us with the truth about the toy industry.

Occult symbols in cartoons are extremely prevalent. I feel the heat of spiritual warfare as I stretch out my arm and turn off the TV. I sense conflict in the tense atmosphere among the disgruntled children. Freedom from my spiritual enemies is my choice.

In everything – in all circumstances – Paul the apostle exhorts us to give thanks. In the desert. In our low estate. In combat with our enemies.

Verse 25 depicts God as the provider *"who gives food to every creature."*

I suggest we don't wait to say a nicely worded prayer of thanks at a laden table on Christmas Day. Let's thank God, as we stand in line in the supermarket. We could thank Him for each item in the grocery cart; for the friends and relations we've invited over; for all the blessings God, our caregiver, showers on us.

The last verse of Psalm 136 reads: *"Give thanks to the God of Heaven."*

The Psalmist has come full circle. Eyes off the gifts. Eyes on the Giver. Praising God, not for what He does, but for Who He is.

Who is He? He's the almighty, omnipotent, omniscient, omnipresent God of heaven, who encouragingly beckons to us through the desert. The compassionate God of heaven, who weeps with us, in our low estate. The victorious God of heaven, who fights, and frees us from our enemies. He's the great creator God. The God of gods. Lord of lords. The GOOD God.

Every day I face a choice – to grumble or to be grateful. To protest or to praise. To complain or compose a psalm. I choose Psalm 151.

NEVER MEANS NEVER, BUT ONLY UNTIL GRACE STEPS IN

The cry of a newborn baby echoes around the damp walls of the smelly cave. Wrapping him in a strip of stained cloth, his mother hands him to his father, her own father – Lot. Motherly pride is tainted with shame; she avoids eye contact with the old man and whispers her son's name: Moab.

*** *** ***

The woman peers into the small mirror and puts the finishing touches to her red lips; carefully she adds a little more eyeliner to her left eye. Then, satisfied with her looks, she relaxes on the cushions placed invitingly on her bed.

Frantic banging on the door startles her. Clients at this time of day? She hurries to attend them.

They are not the usual type of men who visit a harlot. Instinctively, she knows they are on a different mission and she is withdrawn, almost afraid. Her conversation with them reveals her true heart, her awe and respect for their God.

"I know that the Lord has given you this land and that a great fear of you has fallen on us, so that all who live in this country are melting in fear because of you. We have heard how the Lord dried up the water of the Red Sea for you when you came out of Egypt, and what you did to

Sihon and Og, the two kings of the Amorites east of the Jordan, whom you completely destroyed. When we heard of it, our hearts melted in fear and everyone's courage failed because of you, for the Lord your God is God in heaven above and on the earth below" (Joshua 2:9).

Rahab is a believer in the one true God, presumably untainted by the dangerously contaminating beliefs of the inhabitants of her town, Jericho.

*** *** ***

Ruth knows her roots. The ancestral stigma of incest drapes around her shoulders like an unclean cloth. Does she know the Israelite law?

"Therein was found written that the Ammonite and the Moabite should not come into the congregation of God, ever" (Deuteronomy 23:3).

At the bend of the road, the Moabite widow pauses briefly. Her mind made up, she will not turn back.

"Where you go I will go, and where you stay I will stay. Your people will be my people and your God my God" (Ruth 1:16).

She shoulders her bag of belongings, and without a backward glance, falls into step with her mother-in law. A new land awaits her, new laws, new customs.

Those customs are strange to Ruth, and she struggles to comprehend the role of a redeemer. Nevertheless, lack of understanding doesn't hinder the marvellous result. Her unsavoury and shameful ancestry is covered with the cloak of her redeemer. The offer of marriage to a wealthy kinsman changes the course of her life.

The day arrives when she meets her new mother-in-law.

"Sit here my daughter."

The elderly woman beckons the nervous bride-to-be. They sit together and share their life stories.

"I am here," her new mother-in-law begins, "only and solely by the grace of God, the Israelites' God. He has removed the shame of my past and given me a future. What He's done for me, He will do for you."

Slowly, deliberately she unwraps her sordid beginnings. She misses no detail. Here is a Canaanite harlot who has found and who delights in the pure, unadulterated grace of God. She tells of her rescue from Jericho, her life lived among the Israelites, then finally of her marriage to Salmon and the birth of Boaz.

Tears spring to Ruth's eyes.

Rahab reaches across and squeezes her hand.

"It's all about grace," she whispers.

Re-telling her story has renewed the reality of the miracle. Tears of gratitude trickle down her wrinkled cheeks.

The two non-Israelite women sit, arms wrapped around one another. Once banned, ostracised, and cruelly criticised, they now weep for sheer joy.

Accepted, because of grace.

The God of all grace, who knows the end from the beginning, looks on and smiles. He already knows **what** will be written about them some 4000 years later. He knows **where** their names will be included, and **why.**

*"This is the genealogy of Jesus the Messiah the son of David, the son of Abraham: "... Salmon the father of Boaz, whose mother was **Rahab**, Boaz the father of Obed, whose mother was **Ruth**, Obed the father of Jesse, and Jesse the father of King David.... and Jacob the father of Joseph, the husband of Mary, and Mary was the mother of **Jesus** who is called the Messiah"* (Matthew 1:1-16).

Never means never, but only until GRACE steps in.

STRESS IS STRESSFUL

The young zebra twitched nervously. Lame, and unable to keep up with the rest of the herd, he stood exhausted and alone in the fierce midday heat.

A dry twig snapped under his feet. He glanced down. His throat constricted as he saw a thin black thread. A snake? His neck muscles tightened and his eyes narrowed as suspiciously he watched it ripple along the stones. It stretched longer. And longer.

The big striped animal trembled. This was no snake. A furtive glance at his bare white rump revealed to him the horrifying truth. He was losing his stripes.

The caption over this sketch reads: *"I think I'm losing my stripes."*

Stress is fast becoming a popular scapegoat, the legitimate excuse for our moods and reactions. Webster's dictionary defines it as "A factor causing mental and emotional strain or tension; the physical and mental state resulting from such strain."

Interruptions cause stress.

In his article, *Surrendering to the Interruptions,* Joseph M. Stowell, president of the Moody Bible Institute, comments that even happy interruptions ultimately cause havoc. Bane or blessing, interruptions always have a way of shredding a person's day.

It is the shredding that causes stress.

For me, a missionary in Colombia, just living is stressful. The media refer to it as one of the most violent countries in the world. They interrupt the TV programmes with news flashes, thrusting violence into our living room. However, these interruptions don't affect us as much as the daily happenings.

Our children troop happily off to school. They return an hour later and announce: "The teachers are on strike." Our day and their day has been shredded.

I reach the head of a 35-minute queue in the bank. "You can't draw out any money at the moment. Our communication system is out of order," the poker-facer teller, informs me. My plans are interrupted.

I have a deadline to meet; a Bible lesson to prepare. Someone rings the doorbell. My plans are put on hold, my schedule interrupted. Like the zebra, I experience stress.

Did Jesus experience stress? I believe He did. *"He Himself has fully shared in all our experience of temptation, except that He never sinned,"* is J B Phillip's translation of Hebrews 4:14.

Max Lucado writes about "the second most stressful day in the life of Jesus" in his book, *In the Eye of the Storm*. It is the day He gets news of His cousin John's death; the disciples then unburden themselves after their preaching tour. Jesus suggests a mini-holiday, but someone spots them as their boat leaves. They arrive to find the place crowded, and Jesus spends the rest of the day teaching and healing. Late afternoon, He organises a meal for over five thousand people.

By His reactions to these stressful situations, Jesus shows us how to cope with stress. Mark 6:31 reads: *"So many people were coming and going that they did not have a chance to eat."*

That describes our home. Some days the visitors just keep coming. We stretch the meal. Everyone gets something.

Jesus, aware of their predicament, invited His disciples to take time out with Him. Their welfare was important to Him. Others first. That was His attitude in a stressful situation.

Never had a boat trip been so pleasurable, as they anticipated a day of relaxation together, alone.

I recall the day an elderly man telephoned us to ask whether he could bring his wife and teenage daughter, to spend a week's holiday at our place. Ours was not a guesthouse. It was a home for 15 children from dysfunctional families. My caller suffered from his nerves. His wife was partially deaf and had a peptic ulcer. Inside, I heard the answer screaming. *No!*

When Jesus and His overtaxed disciples arrived at the nice quiet place, it was full of people. Nervy people. Partially deaf people. People with sour faces and problems.

The disciples must have held their breath and watched Jesus to see how He would cope.

The New English Bible says: *"His heart went out to them"* (Mark 4:38).

I would have avoided stress if I had reacted to my caller in the same way: with compassion.

The disciples' rest-day turned into an all-day teaching seminar. By late afternoon, they were keen to dismiss the crowd. Jesus responded with love. He went straight ahead and arranged an impromptu picnic.

Not only did five thousand men *"eat to their hearts' content"* (Mark 6:42 NEB), but also countless thousands are still receiving blessing through reading this miracle. Blessing results when we respond with love.

I still smile when I think about the change we saw in the nervy little man and his sour-faced wife. He relaxed, and she discovered the art of looking on the funny side of things. We all laughed a lot that week.

Getting our priorities right can help us cope with stress.

Mark 6:45 shows Jesus' priorities. *"After the picnic was over, He dispatched the disciples in the boat. He then dismissed the crowd. Then He went up on a mountainside to pray."*

Jesus needed that communication with His Father, but He put His own need last.

In their book, *Ministering Cross-culturally,* the authors, Sherwood G Lingenfelter and Marvin K Mayers, discuss the need to maintain a balance between being task-oriented and people-oriented. They emphasise that no goal or task of ours, is of greater importance than the people to whom God has sent us to minister.

Max Lucado reminds us that people are precious. To use his illustration, when they all crowd round to have a piece of us like piranhas in the Amazon River, we will be able to cope better if we remember Jesus' attitude: people are precious.

Joseph Stowell suggests we see every interruption as a divinely scheduled event for His glory and gain.

A divinely scheduled event. I'm trying that outlook. There's less stress, even when I feel I'm losing my stripes like the nervous young zebra.

THAT SUBTLE SHIFT – PART 1

"Look out! There's another one!"

In the desperate scuffle, bodies fall over one another in an attempt to escape, but it is too late.

Mesmerised, the boy stares at the two red dots on his ankle. A scream forms in his throat. He opens his mouth but no sound comes. A curse splits the air. Someone stabs viciously at the snake, misses it, and curses again.

Unobtrusively, the snake slides silently on to its next victim, a toddler playing in the sand. Her tiny body twitches violently, and then suddenly slumps forward.

As the venomous reptiles slither in and out of the tents, the wailing of the bereaved mingles with the shrieking of the victims.

Verse 6 of Numbers chapter 21 states bluntly: *"They bit the people and many Israelites died."*

"Look at it! Look at it and live!"

The hysterical weeping ceases, as the bitten believe. They look, and they live.

This is what God said to Moses: *"Make a snake and put it up on a pole; anyone who is bitten can look at it and live"* (Numbers 21:8).

So what brought life to the dying? Simple belief in God's provision. Implicit belief in what He said. Profound belief in God Himself.

Did some think it too simple? Or too ridiculous? We aren't told. We read: *"... when anyone was bitten by a snake and looked at the bronze snake, he lived"* (Numbers 21:9).

I sense a tremendous sigh between those words in verse 9 and the next phrase in verse 10: *"The Israelites moved on."*

A sigh, because the terror of snakebite is behind them; because relief has come; because an angry Yahweh has in His great mercy provided a way to life. They sigh for the dead they have left buried in the sand. And they move on.

I stop here and ask some questions: "Before they moved on, who took the pole down? Who decided whether they would take the bronze snake with them, or leave it behind? Did they take it with them? Why would they want to take it with them?"

Perhaps my questions are not important. But move on with the Israelites several hundred years down the track, and we face another question. This one *is* important.

At what point in time did they begin to worship the bronze snake?

2 Kings 18 relates Hezekiah's encounter with this bronze snake. Verse 4 reads: *"He broke into pieces the bronze snake Moses had made, for up to that time the Israelites had been burning incense to it."*

Blatant idolatry.

The previous chapter gives us a clue to this horrendous situation: *"Even while these people were worshipping the Lord, they were serving their idols."*

It happens ever so subtly when *what*, or *how*, or even *when*, become more important than WHOM. It happens when the eyes of the heart shift their gaze to the visible.

Could our emphasis of a particular doctrine take our eyes off the Lord Himself?

Could 'anointed teaching' replace a personal relationship with the Anointed One?

Could truths deceive us into believing that they are more important than the Truth?

Is it possible to worship 'worship'?

Could the *way* we do things override the *why* or *what for*?

Could a 'man of God' shift our eyes off God? Switch our focus from the invisible to the visible?

THAT SUBTLE SHIFT – PART 2

Three hundred clay jars crash.

Three hundred trumpets blast.

The sound sends chills of fear through the hearts of the Midianites down in the valley below.

It sends thrills of victory through the hearts of the Israelites on the surrounding hills. As one man they yell: *"A sword for the Lord and for Gideon"* (Judges 7:20).

Gideon remembers the day he was commissioned. The words still ring in his ears: *"The Lord is with you, mighty warrior"* (Judges 6:12).

This is Gideon, the well-known hero we admired in Sunday School.

We first meet him, receiving a visit from God Himself, who names him 'mighty warrior', assures him of His very presence and then commissions him to save Israel. This is Jerub-Baal who valiantly demolishes Baal's altar, and who then works alongside God, in the selection of soldiers for his army. This is Gideon who wins a war with a shout.

Everyone talked about Gideon. Some praised him, some berated him, but no matter what they said about him, his name fast became a household word. The townsfolk in Ophrah lifted his name high above their heads like some golden trophy. The seventy-seven officials of Succoth cursed him while their wives poured oil on their scratched and bleeding backs. The widows of Peniel whispered his name to their sobbing children. The Israelites openly flattered him. "Rule over us," they begged.

Gideon was famous. As a warrior, his conduct was blameless. If he were alive today, his name would be on the New Year's honours list. The twenty-first century church would refer to him as 'a man of God'.

Gideon, why did you do it?

We can only speculate, as we read and re-read the tragic events that follow the chronicles of his spectacular army career. Gideon, your hero image is totally ruined, tarnished beyond repair.

When did that subtle shift occur in Gideon's heart?

With his lips, he nobly refused the offer of kingship, but in the next breath asked for a king's bounty.

Did the tinkle of hundreds of gold earrings, cascading onto the folds of cloth, send quivers of emotion through Gideon's heart? Did the glint of those hundreds of gold earrings in the bright sunlight, blind his eyes to the shaft of greed that penetrated his heart at that precise moment?

Judges chapter 8 verse 27 paints a dark picture of this man and his newly acquired gold. *"Gideon made the gold into an ephod."*

An ephod was part of the priestly garments worn by those who ministered in the Lord's presence. But this ephod would never be used for that purpose.

Could a 'man of God' shift our eyes off God?

"All Israel prostituted themselves by worshipping it there" (Judges 8:27).

The ephod made by Gideon became the focus of their worship. Their focus shifted from the invisible to the visible.

Blatant idolatry. So subtle. So devastatingly destructive. The shattering consequences wreaked havoc in the lives of his sons, in the lives of his grandchildren and in all the following generations.

I stop here and ask myself some questions:

Where are the eyes of my heart?

Could my emphasis of a particular doctrine, take my eyes off the Lord Himself?

Do I permit 'anointed teaching' to replace my personal relationship with the Anointed One?

Which truths deceive me into believing that they are more important than the Truth?

Do I worship 'worship'?

Could the way I do things, override the why or what for?

Could a 'man of God' shift my eyes off God? Switch my focus from the invisible to the visible?

"Lord, I lift my eyes and look at You. Doctrine slips into focus when I have a close relationship with You. You, the Anointed One are my personal teacher. Human truth pales into insignificance when I believe You; it's what You say about me that counts. Teach me what it means to worship You 24/7. Switch my focus from the visible to

You the Invisible. **It's all about You Lord.** In You I live and move and have my being."

THERE CAN ONLY BE ONE ANSWER

The woman of my dreams!

Dave places the remote control on his bedside table and stretches out on the bed. Closing his eyes, he allows a re-play of the video scenes to dance before him.

His mobile phone rings. Dave glances at the name, and silences it. The last thing he wants right now, is news of the war.

Lazily he rolls off the bed and serves himself a whisky. He doesn't feel inclined to do anything, so putting on his sunglasses, he steps out on to the balcony. He's offered a great view from the 10th floor.

Leaning on the rails, he sips his drink and allows his imagination to re-visit the final scenes of the video. Suddenly he stiffens. His vision blurs.

Dave removes his sunglasses and passes his hand in front of his eyes. No, it's not his imagination. A female form slides out of the swimming pool on the penthouse terrace in the apartments across the road.

A discharge of adrenaline drives the man to grab his mobile phone and connect with a friend.

"Hi. Would you do me a favour?"

He breathes deeply and comes straight to the point. "You remember the apartments across the road from me? Ask the guard on duty the name of the blonde girl who lives in the penthouse. Then get back to me."

Barely five minutes later, he receives the answer.

"Sheba. Sergeant Ryan's wife."

Dave, a man well versed in war strategies, switches off his mobile phone and begins to devise an elaborate strategy to seduce the girl.

That very evening, Sheba steps out of the elevator straight into Dave's cleverly woven trap. He is wearing brightly coloured Bermuda shorts and casual footwear carefully chosen for the occasion. Taken aback by his effusive welcome, she accepts a drink. The romantic music and the man's amorous behaviour subtly hypnotise her, and as night falls, the two drift into the bedroom.

*** *** ***

Several weeks later Dave sees an unknown number on the screen of his mobile phone. Two missed calls from the same number arouse his curiosity. The phone blinks. It's the same number.

The news hits him; the bullet has found its mark. Dave collapses onto the sofa clutching at his stomach. The result of that romantic encounter will make an appearance in nine months' time, with two eyes, a nose and a mouth.

The victim of that bullet sits for a long time. When he stands up, he has everything planned to the last detail. Before going to bed, he makes a brief phone call.

"Send me Sergeant Ryan on the first flight out tomorrow."

Dave dispatches his personal chauffeur to meet him at the airport and has him brought to the apartment. The two converse amicably over a glass of whisky. Ryan relaxes and shares the latest information about the war. Several glasses later, Dave suggests the soldier goes home to his wife.

"Take the rest of the day off, young man. Your wife will have been missing you."

Next morning the news reaches Dave that Ryan is back at the army base. He didn't go home. This complicates the situation but doesn't faze Dave. He puts into action his backup plan.

Step-by-step he carries out that plan, sending the sergeant on a complicated and dangerous mission. It is no surprise to Dave when he receives the news. Ryan is dead.

The plan worked. Dave takes Sheba to be his wife and together they await the birth of their son.

So far it's all wrong. It must not be minimised. It's adultery. It's sin.

Dave lives the bitter consequences: his baby son takes sick and dies.

The devastated father truly repents, receives God's forgiveness and moves on.

The end of the matter. Chapter closed.

Or is it?

I'm looking at 2 Samuel chapter 12 verse 24. This is going to need a bit of explaining. *"Then David comforted his wife Bathsheba, and he went to her and made love to her. She gave birth to a son, and they named him Solomon. The Lord loved him; and because the Lord loved him, he sent word through Nathan the prophet to name him Jedidiah."*

Why? Why? Why? The word screams in my head.

I have questions. They are tough questions that demand answers.

Why did the Lord specially love **this** *baby, after the episode of blatant sin?*

Why didn't He choose the son of one of David's other wives, to be heir to the throne?

Why is this woman included in the genealogy of Jesus Christ?

I can't come up with an explanation. I believe it has something to do with the apostle Paul's observation: *"But where sin increased and abounded, grace (God's unmerited favour) has surpassed it and increased the more and superabounded"* (Romans 5:20 AMPC).

There can only be one answer.

In the very area David failed…

I see GRACE, super abounding GRACE.

WHEN NO HELP COMES

Moses finds himself in a desperate situation: in charge of several million people, a colossal army behind him, and an immense stretch of water in front. He asks God's help. Is it not justifiable to ask help from God in such a difficult situation?

Along with Moses, let's listen to the unexpected reply. It sounds more like a list of instructions:

*"Why do you cry to **Me**?*

***Tell** the children of Israel to go forward.*

But lift up your rod and stretch out your hand over the sea and divide it…" (Exodus 14:15-16 NKJV).

The moment has come for Moses to exercise his faith. His authority is his rod, the instrument given by God, the sign of His presence and power. God had said to him: *"And be sure to take your rod along so that you can perform the miracles I have shown you"* (Exodus 4:17 TLB).

As Moses takes action, he honours God and shows he believes in the authority given to him to perform miracles. In the earthly realm it's not God who divides the sea. It's Moses. He has the authority. He stretches out his hand and divides the sea because his faith activates God's power.

Sometimes when I ask God for His help it seems I receive no reply, or not the reply I want.

Now I understand why there are occasions when God doesn't answer my plea for help; it's simply because He has already answered and is waiting for me to exercise my faith and go ahead! If I believe, I will take action.

"Lord, I confess that at times I use prayer as a refuge to dodge the action of faith. I decide to believe that in Christ Jesus, You have given me Your authority to do Your will. I lift up the rod, (the authority You have given me), and in the Name of Jesus Christ, I stretch out my hand and divide the sea. I believe and take action."

WOUNDED BY ONE OF JESUS' FOLLOWERS

"Tonight He'll be captured. One of His followers will show you where."

Malchus receives his master's curt order in silence and in so doing becomes an innocent pawn in the most cowardly conspiracy of all history.

Night falls and a detachment of soldiers, together with several officials, meet together. Malchus joins them. He looks around and notices that some of the company carry arms, others hold flaming torches. A man hurries up to them and makes signs that they follow him.

The group hastens to keep up with him as he takes them along a dark alleyway that leads to the Kidron Valley. They enter a garden. The low branches of the trees brush their faces, but they push ahead, blazing torches held high, arms at the ready. From the rear, Malchus stretches up, curious to see the man he has heard so much about. He is surprised to see Him walk out of the shadows and ask them a question.

"Who is it you want?"

"Jesus of Nazareth," shout several of the group.

"I am He."

On hearing that, the group, including the traitor, take a step backwards and tumble to the ground. Kicking and cursing they somehow get back on their feet and Malchus finds himself beside Jesus who repeats the question.

"Who is it you want?"

The reply is repeated.

"Jesus of Nazareth."

Malchus holds his breath and gazes at the man's face.

"I told you that I am He."

In the moments that follow, there is total confusion. Shouts and curses fill the air. Suddenly Malchus and one of Jesus' followers find themselves the protagonists in the ensuing chaotic scene.

In the light of the flaming torches, a sword flashes, taking Malchus by surprise. Bewildered, he quickly turns his head and the blade falls on his right ear. Malchus reaches up and feels the blood run down his cheek. Time seems to stand still. For a brief moment, an uncanny silence descends on the group. Jesus touches Malchus' ear. For a second their eyes meet.

The high priest's servant touches his ear gingerly. He finds it completely healed.

*** *** ***

The news quickly spreads.

"The high priest's servant has been wounded."

"His ear was cut off. Anyone know who did it?"

A woman interrupts the conversation.

"I don't believe it. I saw Malchus this morning and both his ears were firmly in place."

A young fellow joins the group of gossipers.

"I know who did it! One of the followers of that man Jesus."

"How come? You mean one of the followers of the Master from Galilee, wounded someone?"

The murmuring swells like a wave of the sea.

"Someone wounded Malchus!"

"It was one of Jesus' followers!"

"His ear was cut off!"

A teenager runs towards the group and interrupts the gossip.

"I've got the hot news! It's incredible!"

He stops to regain his breath.

"Hey listen… Malchus is healed… It was like this… Jesus put out His hand… and He touched his ear… and like I said… Malchus was healed… and what's more… I saw him this morning!"

The boy runs off to spread the good news to everyone he meets.

"Hey listen… Jesus healed Malchus!"

The good news is for us too: Jesus heals wounds… every kind of wound… including emotional wounds… and yes… even a wound like Malchus suffered… a wound inflicted by a follower of Jesus Christ.

STORYTIME

So that you can know and understand what is the
immeasurable and unlimited and surpassing greatness
of His power in and for us who believe.

Ephesians 1:19 AMPC

ISHMAEL NEVER ENJOYED GOD'S PRESENCE

"An angel spoke to me! He spoke to me, an Egyptian woman, a mere slave!"

Hagar, totally exhausted, sank to her knees in the hot sand. There was so much to think about, and she needed time to recover. She had just had an encounter with an angel. Yes, an angel had spoken to her. She tried to collect her confused thoughts and think back over the traumatic events of her life. Her relationship with Abram had been for convenience, of that she was certain. He needed an heir. Sarai's words to her husband were engraved in her memory: *"Go, sleep with my maidservant; perhaps I can build a family through her"* (Genesis 6:12).

Hagar shuddered and placed a hand over the bulge that was her baby. Her baby? Or was he Sarai's baby? She wasn't sure. She felt used, unloved. Cheated, unappreciated. From the day she realised she was pregnant, things had gone from bad, to worse. She despised her mistress. Terrible feelings had begun to twist themselves around her wounded heart: anger, hate, low self-esteem, resentment, rebelliousness. And without her realising it, all these feelings had been transmitted to her unborn child.

Hagar tried to recall every detail of what the angel had said.

The baby was to be named Ishmael which means 'God hears', because He had heard of her misery. This child would be against everyone and everyone would be against him, free and untamed as a wild donkey.

Hagar frowned. *He's going to be a handful,* she mused.

But the most annoying part of the conversation was the angel's instruction to go back to her mistress, back to the beatings and the insults. It wasn't fair. Her eyes filled with tears she was too proud to let fall, and in that moment a seed was sown in her wounded, resentful heart: the seed of bitterness.

Dizzily, Hagar struggled to her feet. Thoughts swirled round in her aching head like the hot sand that swirled round her tired feet. Reluctantly, she began to walk.

After walking for a long time, the slave woman arrived at the campsite that was the only home she remembered. She took a deep breath, bowed her head and stepped inside the tent of her mistress.

*** *** ***

And so Ishmael was born. As Abram took his firstborn in his arms, he felt a strange uneasiness. Looking down at the tiny face with distinctive Egyptian features, he asked himself: *Is this the promised child? Is this my heir?* Somehow, he felt he had taken a wrong turn in his effort to help God keep His promise of an heir and numerous descendants. But in spite of the doubts that clouded what should have been a moment of intense joy, Abram felt a surge of deep love for his son. The old man sighed as he tenderly kissed the baby's forehead.

*** *** ***

"Get out of my way. Get out of the tent." The old woman pushed the toddler towards the opening.

"Go and lie down. I told you not to get up from your mat," shouted a tall, dark woman as she shoved him back from the tent opening.

Totally frustrated, the child threw himself on the ground and screamed, his protests mingling with the angry voices of the two women as they insulted one another.

The tent flap moved and an elderly man stepped inside. Immediately the tirade ceased. The two women lowered their heads and their voices. The old man bent down and picked up his small son, still kicking and screaming.

From the security of his father's arms the child looked from one woman to the other and scowled. Then, leaning his head on his father's shoulder, he stuck two chubby fingers in his mouth and closed his eyes to his hostile surroundings. In the dreadful confusion, one thing was clear in his baby mind: for some reason he was to blame for the constant conflict.

*** *** ***

Lying on the sand, Ishmael gazed up into the sky. That afternoon he had overheard his father talking to some friends, telling them what Ishmael called, *The Star Story*. He didn't like that story, but if someone had asked him why, he wouldn't have been able to explain. He had heard it so many times that he could repeat it from memory. And each time he heard it, an arrow pierced his heart.

The little boy crossed his arms under his head and imitating his father's voice began to recite. *"What do you think of this my friends, the Lord took me outside and said 'Look up into the heavens and count the stars if you can. Your descendants will be like that – too many to count'"* (Genesis 15:5 TLB).

In the growing darkness, tiny points of light began to appear and, to him, each star represented one of his father's descendants. Ishmael shivered. Suddenly he felt terribly alone and confused. If he was his father's son, why did he always feel he wasn't the main character in the story? Stretching up his arms, he lifted an imaginary bow and began to shoot arrows, in a futile attempt to switch off the hundreds of tiny lights.

*** *** ***

"Did you hear that? Sarah is pregnant!"

"What? That just can't be true!"

"Who? Which Sarah?"

"The one who used to be called Sarai."

"That ninety-year-old woman? Now that is news!"

"They are saying that he's the son of a promise, and that he is the true heir."

From tent to tent, from family to family, the news spread like a fire out of control.

Ishmael didn't join in the excitement. The news confirmed to him what he had long suspected. He was a mistake. The comments about the true heir stabbed him like a sharp knife and he flinched involuntarily each time he heard them. The reality was too painful to accept and the boy grew sullen and bad tempered, refusing to accept every attempt his father made to demonstrate his love for his firstborn.

*** *** ***

The cry of a newborn baby broke the silence. Ishmael heard it and his heart missed a beat. The sound came from the direction of Sarah's tent. He closed his hands into two fists and began to hit the sacks of corn his father had placed in the shade of a tree. Over and over again, he hit the sacks until the corn spilled out at his feet. He stamped on it furiously. Then he kicked the puppy that frolicked beside him and marched out of the campsite. He didn't understand what was happening; he didn't understand his feelings. He hated everyone and most of all he hated that baby.

*** *** ***

Through the years, the bitterness in Ishmael's heart grew silently and undetected like a poisonous gas. Sometimes he felt he would explode. Sometimes he exploded.

"Dad, I need to know the truth."

The 14-year-old shot a defiant glance at the two women in his life. They were squabbling as usual.

"Dad, tell me. Which of those two women is my mother?" His tone was sarcastic. It was obvious he was trying to make his father angry. Through narrowed eyes he watched as Abraham placed a protecting hand on baby Isaac's head. Reluctantly the old man shifted his gaze from the face of his newborn son, to that of the angry teenager.

"Why have you changed your name, Dad?"

Then, putting his hands on his hips, he threw back his head and spat out the question he had reserved for this moment.

"What's so special about this baby?"

Abraham turned his full attention to his firstborn. Patiently and lovingly, he went back to the beginning.

"My son," he began, "that day when God and I spoke together, I said *'If only Ishmael might live under your blessing!'* And God told me there *is* a blessing for you. Listen to what God said about you. *'As for Ishmael, I have heard you: I will surely bless him; I will make him fruitful and will greatly increase his numbers. He will be the father of twelve rulers and I will make him into a great nation'"* (Genesis 17:18, 20).

Ishmael wasn't satisfied. His father's detailed explanation and his affirmation of his love for him, did nothing to appease the anger that burned in his chest. It threatened to suffocate him, along with the hatred, the bitterness and the rejection already firmly entrenched there. His lip curled in contempt.

"Baby Isaac. Huh. The fulfilment of a promise? The son of the covenant? The heir? How dare he be born, horrid little brat! I hate him!"

*** *** ***

The day of Isaac's weaning party arrived. From a distance, Ishmael watched his little brother, the centre of attention. The pain of rejection made him feel terribly alone.

"I don't belong here. They are a family. I'm an outsider."

Suddenly, the adrenaline of vengeance raced through his veins driving him to make a decision. This was the perfect moment: Ishmael went up to his little brother and began mocking him in front of all the guests.

Like an avalanche of rocks that appeared from nowhere, Sarah's reaction to Ishmael's behaviour took all the guests by surprise. Heads turned. Mouths opened. Eyebrows went up. Sarah the perfect hostess, inexplicably threw herself on her husband.

Each word, a stone thrown with tremendous force, hit and wounded the heart of Ishmael's father.

"Get rid of that slave woman and her son, for that slave woman's son will never share in the inheritance with my son Isaac" (Genesis 21:10).

Abraham was most distressed. This was about his own son. The old man spent a sleepless night, his only comfort God's words: *"It is through Isaac that your offspring will be reckoned. I will make the son of the maidservant into a nation also, because he is your offspring"* (Genesis 21:13).

Early next morning Ishmael watched in disbelief as his father filled a skin with water and packed a basket of food. He was conscious of a dreadful sinking feeling in his stomach. OK, he had been rude to his spoilt little brother, but would his father kick him out of the family just for that? A searing pain shot through his heart as the root of bitterness twisted itself into a knot. Hot, angry tears spilled down his cheeks.

Abraham placed the skin of water and the food on Hagar's shoulders, but Ishmael carried a heavier burden. He carried his reactions to the deception, and the injustice he had suffered even from before he was born. He carried the burden of guilt, anxiety, anger and resentment; he would carry this burden for the rest of his life.

His father called him, said goodbye and handed him over to his birth mother. In total silence, the teenager walked out into the desert behind her.

*** *** ***

"There isn't any more water."

Hagar's words sank like a heavy stone into Ishmael's semi-conscious mind. Every Bedouin knew that without water, survival in the desert was impossible. Lying faint under a bush, he began to cry, the sobs breaking out from the depths of his being, cracking open the hard shell that had formed around his heart. Pent up anger, frustration and bitterness spilled out. He ran his tongue over his parched lips and tasted the salt from his tears. Wearily he closed his eyes to his hostile surroundings.

Later he woke to feel a trickle of water running down his throat. He swallowed and tried to focus on what his mother was saying.

"God heard you," she whispered. "He heard you crying and showed me where to get water. He said that He will make a great nation from your descendants. Take courage, Ishmael. I know for sure that God is with you."

Yes, God **was** with Ishmael but his bitterness did not permit him to enjoy His presence.

*** *** ***

Ishmael grew up and became an expert archer. He no longer shot imaginary arrows into the sky to put out the stars. Every arrow that hit its mark, strengthened the root of bitterness that not only filled his heart, but like a malignant tumour, spread through his being and controlled his life. His mother remembered the angel's words: *"He will be a wild donkey of a man; his hand will be against everyone and everyone's hand against him, and he will live in hostility towards all his brothers* (Genesis 16:12).

*** *** ***

Standing in the door of his tent, Ishmael looked towards the horizon at the cloud of dust. Visitors? No one ever visited Ishmael, a solitary man, isolated in his own emotional desert. Not even his twelve adult children felt at home with him. The cloud of dust grew larger and as Ishmael made out the forms of two camels, his curiosity also grew.

"Uncle! Uncle Ishmael! It's me, your nephew. I'm Esau…"

Esau? Isaac's son? Ishmael wiped the sweat from his brow; his heart was beating fast as he swallowed hard. But his fear had no grounds. Within a very short time the two men found the link that united their souls. They had something in common; they understood one another. For the first time in his life, Ishmael could express his bitterness to someone who understood him completely.

*** *** ***

Many years went by. The two brothers, Isaac and Ishmael found themselves side by side in front of their father Abraham's grave. Death, that inevitable, bitter fact, had united them for a brief moment. Did they look at each other? Did they speak to one another? Did they attempt reconciliation? I don't know. But what is certain is that to this day, Isaac's descendants and Ishmael's descendants are still in disagreement. The chain of bitterness stretches on from generation to generation. The Jews and the Arabs are still enemies in the twenty first century.

And how did Ishmael's life end?

He died without receiving God's promised blessing, without enjoying His presence; he never released and handed over to God that heavy burden of reactions to life's adverse circumstances.

He died as he was born: bitter.

ESAU, SCARRED BY DECEPTION

"Isaac! Isaac! Good news!"

Rebekah ran towards her husband, threw her arms around his neck, and buried her face in his beard.

"God has heard our prayer."

Isaac looked into her eyes.

"Thank God," he whispered. "We're going to have a child!"

Their happiness was short-lived. Rebekah's pregnancy became increasingly difficult. She asked God about the situation and His answer surprised her.

"The sons in your womb shall become two rival nations. One will be stronger than the other, and the older shall be a servant of the younger."

Confused, Rebekah shook her head.

Sure enough, Rebekah had twins.

The first was born covered with what appeared to be a hairy red coat.

"His name is Esau," those present decided, as they looked at the squirming little body, because the word Esau sounds a little like the Hebrew word for hair.

The second baby was born with one hand clutching Esau's heel. To remember that curious happening, the folk gave him the name Jacob, which in Hebrew means simply, "he grabs the heel."

*** *** ***

"Gonna tell Mum!"

Little Jacob stuck out his foot, tripped up his brother, and ran off laughing.

"As if I care! Gonna tell Dad!"

Indignant, Esau struggled to his feet and brushed the dust off his hairy little legs. Running to where his father sat, he scrambled up on to his knee and blurted out his grievance. His father's response made everything right in a few seconds. The little boy grinned. He knew he could count on dad to defend him.

The constant infantile fights repeatedly caused trouble between the parents. The mother doted on Jacob, while Esau was dad's favourite. Sadly, their attitude inadvertently strengthened the rivalry between the twins, and even worse, was the potent fertiliser that fed a hidden root of bitterness in the heart of one small member of the family.

The children grew and each developed his own personality. Esau loved the open countryside, his greatest pleasure to hunt and to receive his father's congratulations. Tiredness vanished upon hearing the question:

"Son, what did you bring me today?"

At nightfall, father and son would sit down to enjoy the venison and one another's company.

Jacob, on the other hand, preferred to stay in the camp near his mother. It was no secret that Rebekah loved Jacob more than his twin. From an early age, she taught him to listen to her voice and to obey her, without questioning.

*** *** ***

Jacob whistled as he stirred the contents of the pot. Closing his eyes for a moment, he allowed the provocatively tempting smell of lentil stew to pervade his nostrils.

Suddenly the peace and quiet was interrupted by the noisy arrival of his brother.

"Bother!" Jacob turned and scowled at the source of the noise. "It was quiet and peaceful till you arrived."

"I'm done." Esau threw his bow and quiver to the ground. "Almost impossible to catch anything today."

The hunter wrinkled his nose and sidled up to the pot of lentil stew.

"Serve me," he demanded.

Jacob frowned, but his response was immediate, swift as an arrow aimed at its target.

"OK. Trade me your birthright for it!"

The cook held his breath as he waited for his brother's reaction.

"When a man's dying of starvation, what good's a birthright?"

To emphasise his plight, Esau slumped to the ground and closed his eyes.

Realising that his brother was serious Jacob replied, "Well then, vow to God that it's mine!"

Esau opened his eyes and without thinking twice, swore to him.

"Here, take it." Jacob handed over a bowl of lentil stew and a hunk of bread. Esau savoured every spoonful.

"Must admit you're a good cook," he grunted. "Red lentils are my favourite," he added, wiping his mouth with the back of his hairy hand. From that day on his nickname was *Edom*, meaning 'red'.

*** *** ***

The years passed and Isaac began to lose his sight.

One day he called Esau.

"Son, I'm an old man now and expect to die any day. Go to the field with your bow and arrows and get me some venison. Make me a good stew just the way I like it, and bring it to me to eat. I want to give you the blessing that belongs to you as my eldest son."

Sadness clashed with the joyful anticipation of his long awaited blessing; sadness at the thought of the imminent death of his best friend, his faithful ally, his beloved father. Picking up his bow and arrows, Esau made his way into the open countryside.

Someone moved in the shadows behind the tent, someone who had been listening to the conversation between Isaac and his favourite son. Rebekah quickly called *her* favourite son, Jacob, and told him what she had just heard. She then gave him instructions on how to steal Esau's blessing and how to trick his father.

Jacob had always obeyed his mother's voice without question. Now the only thing that worried him was that his father would discover the lies and curse him rather than bless him. His mother's reply disarmed him. "My son, let the curse fall on me. Just do what I say."

Jacob got the kids, and his mother quickly prepared the stew. Then taking Esau's best clothes, she dressed her younger son. She solved the problem of his hairless arms and neck by covering them with the goatskins, and then as an accomplice in this terrible deception, she handed him the stew and bread and sent him to his father.

The trick was a success and Jacob received the coveted blessing.

Just as Jacob left his father's tent, Esau came in from the field. The long awaited sacred moment was almost a reality. The hunter prepared his father's favourite dish with high expectations, all the while imagining his reaction, his appreciation, his approval. As he put the finishing touches to the meal, he tried to guess what the blessing reserved for him, as the eldest son, would be. His heart raced as he entered his father's tent, the cheerful tone of his voice reflecting his excitement. "Dad, sit up and eat from some of my game. Then you can give me your blessing."

"Who are you?" his father interrupted.

"I'm Esau your firstborn son."

Could it be that the old man was losing his memory as well as his sight? Esau was not prepared for what happened next. The old man began to tremble violently.

"Who was it then, that hunted game and brought it to me?"

Confused, he shook his head and continued,

"I ate it just before you came, and I blessed him."

Esau covered his face with his hands. His heart pounded. Something like acid spilt over inside him, the acid of bitterness, that burns everything it touches.

"Bless me – me too, my father," he wailed.

His father's reply pierced his wounded heart.

"Your brother came deceitfully and took your blessing!"

"He's rightly named Jacob!" The bitter words fell like red hot coals.

"Deceiver! He's fooled me twice. First, my birthright, now my blessing. Have you reserved a blessing for me?"

Isaac remembered the many times he had defended Esau from his brother.

What had been so easy back then, was now impossible.

His pathetic answer only emphasised the reality of the tragedy.

He spoke slowly, each word dripping with hopelessness.

"There's nothing I can do, son. I've already put your brother over you; all his relatives will serve him. I have sustained him with grain and wine. What can I do now for you, my son?"

Waves of anger passed over Esau. His face flushed and his breath came erratically. Clenching his hands, he hunched his trembling body as a bull when faced with a red rag.

"Haven't you one more blessing, my father? Bless me!" he roared. Suddenly he broke down.

Tears rolled down his cheeks, settling into his thick red beard, tears of anger, frustration and helplessness. But instead of relieving the heat inside his chest, the fire intensified and Esau felt the awful effect wrought by the acid of bitterness. Amid his wailing, he heard his father pronounce a 'second class' blessing, or was it a curse?

"Your dwelling will be away from the earth's richness, away from the dew of heaven above. You will live by the sword and you will serve your brother. But when you grow restless, you will throw his yoke from off your neck."

Without even a glance at his father, Esau slunk out of the tent.

"After the mourning for my father's death is over, I will kill Jacob," he muttered.

Rebekah cunningly contrived a plan to protect Jacob. She convinced her husband that the reason was so he would not marry the neighbouring women.

So, with the blessing of his father, Jacob left home.

Apparently this solved the problem. Esau was no longer harassed by his brother's presence, but the bitterness kept eating away inside, influencing all his decisions. He decided to go and visit his Uncle Ishmael.

*** *** ***

"Uncle! Uncle Ishmael! I'm your nephew Esau."

He quickened his steps. Finally he would meet his father's brother, Ishmael, a stranger to the family. He'd heard so much about him and had always had the impression that he was a kindred spirit.

And so it was. Within a very short time the two men found a tie that united their souls. Esau was finally able to express his bitterness to someone who understood him perfectly. Not surprisingly, he fell in love with his cousin Mahalath, Ishmael's daughter; the magnet that drew them together, their bitter outlook on life.

*** *** ***

Years passed. The day came when Esau had the opportunity to reconcile with his brother Jacob, but sadly, hugs and kisses could never eradicate the lasting effect of the bitterness that already pervaded the spiritual DNA of their own children and the following generations.

*** *** ***

Many generations passed.

Obadiah rubs his eyes and wonders if he is dreaming. He shakes his head to convince himself that he is awake. Suddenly it dawns on him that he is witnessing a vision. The prophet of God stands to his feet and gives it all his attention. Adrenaline flows through his body and he begins to speak firmly:

This is what the Sovereign Lord says about Edom: *"See, I will make you small among the nations; you will be utterly despised. The pride of your heart has deceived you, you who live in the clefts of the rocks and make your home on the heights, you who say to yourself, 'Who can bring me down to the ground?' Though you soar like the eagle and make your nest among the stars, from there I will bring you down," declares the Lord. "If thieves came to you, robbers in the night — Oh, what a disaster awaits you! — would they not steal only as much as they wanted? If grape pickers came to you, would they not leave a few grapes? But how Esau will be ransacked, his hidden treasures pillaged! All your allies will force you to the border; your friends will deceive and overpower you; those who eat your bread will set a trap for you..."* (Obadiah 1:1-7).

As the prophet speaks, the details of the Edomites' background become clear; we see beyond the visible, behind the appearances, intentions, and actions.

The endless chain manifests itself in:

- a small redheaded boy, protagonist in a rivalry between twin brothers,
- a teenager, caught in the conflict of parents' preferences,
- a young hunter, victim of his brother's deception,
- a man, caught in a trap set by his own mother,
- a bitter man's affinity for a bitter relative.
- Esau, a link in the chain of bitterness, which perpetuates through his descendants,
- the father of a nation with unbalanced reactions,
- progenitor of a highly aggressive nation,
- a nation that ends up alone, deceived and... annihilated.

Obadiah sighs deeply as he reaches the end of his prophecy. His voice cannot hide his own pain when pronouncing the final words:

"There will be no survivors from Esau. The Lord has spoken" (Obadiah 1:18).

JOSEPH FORGIVES AND THE CHAIN OF BITTERNESS SHATTERS

"My heir!"

The Bedouin gazes at the crumpled face of the tiny creature in his arms. He leans forward and plants a kiss on his forehead.

Strangely, he hadn't felt such strong emotions when Leah's babies were born, or when his concubines Bilhah and Zilpah had given birth. Those women had satisfied his sexual desires, but now Jacob smiles as he remembers the pure joy of intimacy with Rachel, his chosen wife, his beloved.

Not much time passes before the other ten sons are aware that their new brother has a special place in his father's heart; they are annoyed. As they see their father's preference for little Joseph, seeds of envy find fertile soil in the hearts of Simeon, Naphtali, Asher and all the rest.

"Who do you think you are?"

"You have no say here."

"Yeah, I did do it. So what? Ya gonna tell Dad?"

It's obvious. Both words and actions shout: *Joseph we don't like you!* Little Joseph gets his own back, taking tales to his father.

"Daddy, ya know what Judah did? He hit a goat with a stick."

"Dad, Gad tripped me up. Aren't you gonna tell him off?"

As the boys grow, the childish complaints turn into grievances and accusations that demonstrate inconformity, hate and bitterness.

*** *** ***

The atmosphere is tense. The midday heat envelopes the group of Bedouin men squatting in the sparse shade of a tree. Around them, their sheep move restlessly, baa-ing their protests at the temperature, while the men give free rein to their displeasure.

"Did you see the brat this morning?"

"It's beyond belief."

"It's the last straw."

That morning, the old man Jacob had called his favourite son and presented him with a tunic. The tunic is the subject of the conversation under the tree at midday.

"Hey Levi, did you see the tunic?"

"Sure did. It's clear evidence that Father has made him the heir."

"But I'm the firstborn. The tunic belongs to me." Reuben spits on the sand. "Did you see the sleeves?"

"Yeah, and well pointed," replies Simeon. "Just you wait; I'll sort this one out."

Angrily, Simeon leaps to his feet, and clenches his fists. Hoping to see his youngest brother, he glances over to the tents. Vengeance runs through his veins. The truth of the matter is that Reuben has a right to the tunic.

Every Bedouin knows that a tunic that has long pointed sleeves is the gift reserved for the heir.[2] From that day on, the situation between the brothers gets worse; they stop speaking to Joseph. Hatred rears its repulsive head.

One morning Joseph tells the family his strange dream where they all revere him. When a few days later he shares another similar dream, their hatred explodes. Even his father is annoyed and reprimands him, then quietly thinks over the implications. Without a doubt, Joseph is different.

*** *** ***

One day Jacob sends Joseph to visit his brothers who are caring for the flocks in Shechem, little imagining that that very day his sons will retaliate against his favourite boy.

Joseph's brothers see him coming and make their cruel plans to kill him. Reuben doesn't agree. Rather than kill him he suggests throwing him down an empty well.

---

2   Strange Scriptures that Perplex the Western Mind by Barbara Bowen

Joseph arrives and, like a pack of hungry lions, the men fall on him and rip his tunic off him. Grunting and swearing they throw him into the dry well as planned, then satisfied, sit down to enjoy the food their father has sent them.

"Usurper. That's your rightful place."

"Spoiled brat. At last we're rid of him."

"Hey, folks. A caravan's coming. Looks like they're Ishmaelites." Judah has a bright idea. "Let's sell him!"

The next few minutes are a nightmare for Joseph. From the bottom of the pit he is aware of shouting and laughter mixed with the loud complaining of camels. Looking up, he sees mocking faces and barely misses being hit by a rope flung down. He grabs it and is hauled unceremoniously to the surface where he collapses. A violent kick brings him dizzily to his feet.

"Stand up, idiot."

He looks around and the vice of fear grabs his heart. Something terrible is about to take place. He feels a slimy liquid on his shoulder and swings round to come face to face with a ferocious camel. Its breath nauseates him; its saliva revolts him. He steps back and hangs his head.

Incredulous, he listens as the crowd negotiates his life. Amid a heated exchange of words interspersed with oaths, the deal is clinched with twenty silver coins.

Wounded. Betrayed. Sold.

His brothers turn away; the Ishmaelite traders tie his hands and push him towards the caravan. The camel looks on disdainfully and spits again.

*** *** ***

After a humiliating experience in the slave market Joseph arrives at Pharaoh's palace. The following years bring bitter experiences, including a prolonged prison sentence. Victim of a blatant lie, it would be easy to allow this to embitter his heart.

Sitting among the other prisoners Joseph faces a decision: allow himself to become bitter or live in God's presence. Yes, God was with him, the same as he had been with his Great Uncle Ishmael. His decision would influence his future: recognise God's mercy in spite of his adverse circumstances or fill his heart with hatred and vengeance for those who had judged him unjustly.

Joseph closes his eyes and takes a deep breath. The decision is made. Immediately his spirit is freed from the prison of bitterness. He chooses to recognise God's presence in his life. He opens his eyes and no longer sees prison walls; he sees an opportunity to experience true freedom, the sweet nearness of a powerful loving God. He turns and smiles at the prisoner slouching beside him, then gets up to look for the prison warder.

"Sir, how can I help you?"

The free prisoner gives of his best, goes the second mile, and stands out as responsible, honest and kind. Soon the warder puts him in charge of all the prisoners.

Joseph's prison sentence stretches on. Forgotten by a fellow prisoner who had been released unexpectedly, the innocent detainee has every reason to express his indignation, but he has already made his decision; Joseph's heart holds no animosity.

Two long years later, Joseph is called on to interpret a dream. He is freed and promoted to the position of governor of Egypt, at a time when wise management of resources is essential.

*** *** ***

The group of scruffy Bedouins looks out of place in the palace forecourt. They bring their own atmosphere, their own odour. In silence they approach the governor and as is appropriate, bow deeply. The governor stares at them unable to believe his own eyes. His brothers? There's no doubt. His heart thumps and his breath comes in short gasps. Sweat trickles down his temples. His eyes narrow, as he stands erect.

The question comes harshly.

"You, where do you come from?"

He knows the answer. Their accent falls sweetly on his ears. He doesn't need the services of his interpreter.

Huge feathery fans wave lethargically; time seems to stand still. Suddenly Joseph hears the echo of those mocking words: *Do you intend to reign over us? Will you actually rule over us?*

Coming back to the present, Joseph takes charge of the situation. There is an exchange of harsh words. The governor insists they are spies; the Bedouins insist on their innocence. The argument ends with the Bedouins in prison for three days.

The third day, Joseph demands that one of the men remain in custody until the rest return with the youngest, that they have told him about. They converse together about their predicament unaware that the governor understands every word.

Reuben speaks up: "Didn't I tell you not to sin against the boy? But you wouldn't listen. Now we must give an accounting for his blood."

Tears spring unbidden to Joseph's eyes. Turning away, with a great effort he composes himself. Then he gives the order for Simeon to be bound in front of them.

The following orders perplex the servants: some raise their eyebrows; others roll their eyes.

But the orders are carried out:

"Fill the sacks with grain. Return the silver in each sack. Give them provisions for the journey."

*** *** ***

Time passes and the scene repeats itself. The Bedouins arrive at the palace courtyard and reverently bow. The governor barks his orders. "Take these men to my house. Slaughter an animal and prepare dinner. They are to eat with me at noon."

***The chain of bitterness
present in the family from generations behind,
is about to snap!
Love triumphs over evil.***

Joseph arrives home at midday. His brothers bow and give him the gifts they have brought. He asks after their elderly father and then he sees his little brother.

"Is this your youngest brother? God be gracious to you my son."

A tsunami of emotions forces itself into Joseph's heart and threatens to spill over in front of his brothers. He hurries from the room. Throwing himself on to his bed, he sobs inconsolably. Pain, sorrow and nostalgia push for first place in his soul. Instead of bitterness, deep brotherly love floods his whole being.

Seated at the dinner table in their birth order, the brothers glance nervously at one another. No one speaks; their faces reveal consternation and confusion. The food is served them from the governor's table. A question hangs in the air: *Why is Benjamin the youngest being served such exaggerated portions?*

The answer is nearer than they imagine.

*** *** ***

Once again, Joseph orders the money to be returned in the grain sacks and his own silver cup hidden in Benjamin's sack. After dismissing the travellers, he sends someone after them to bring them back in order to investigate the robbery. The culprit will remain as his slave. Judah takes charge of the situation.

"What can we say, my lord? God has uncovered our guilt. We are now your slaves, we ourselves and the one who was found to have the cup."

Joseph's reply hits them like a jet of icy water.

"Not at all. Only the man who was found to have the cup will become my slave. The rest of you, go back to your father in peace."

Judah breaks all the rules of protocol, and goes right up to the stern governor. Joseph listens as the Bedouin speaks at length. He strokes his pointed beard; a slight frown creases his brow. The following offer pierces his heart.

"Please let me stay as your slave. Let the boy go home. How can I go back to my father without him? I can't bear to see my father's misery."

Joseph can no longer control his emotions.

"Make everyone leave my presence," he cries.

Immediately, he breaks down and says, "I am Joseph. Is my father still living?"

His brothers freeze. Some tremble uncontrollably, others go deathly pale. No one dares pronounce a word.

"Come close to me."

In slow motion, the group gathers round.

"I am your brother Joseph, the one you sold to Egypt."

Every eye is on Joseph. Guilt and remorse reflect on their faces.

Joseph continues: "Please don't be distressed, and don't be angry at yourselves for selling me here. It was to save lives that God sent me ahead of you."

***In the spiritual world, a loud noise is heard.
The chain of bitterness from many past generations
is breaking.***

"For two years now there has been famine in the land, and for the next five years there will be no ploughing or reaping. But God sent me ahead of you to preserve for you a remnant on the earth and to save your lives in an extraordinary way. It wasn't you who sent me here, but God."

The sound of men sobbing breaks the thunderous silence that fills the room. Joseph and Benjamin fling their arms around one another weeping. Joseph kisses all his brothers.

Tears flow freely, melting resentment and hatred.

Embraces cause the walls of rivalry to crumble.

Forgiveness shatters the chain of bitterness.

RESCUE OPERATION
AN OUTRAGEOUS SUCCESS

Lucifer grinned. Heaven was in turmoil and all eyes were on him. Well, not all eyes, but at least he had convinced a third of the angelic hosts to worship him. Was not he the most beautiful of all the created beings? Pride oozed and cloaked him with self-enchantment.

Angels were created to worship God; to worship in service and in song. As created beings the relationship they had with God depended on their decision to worship him. They needed to worship in order to maintain that relationship, although God, being God, didn't *need* their worship.

But Lucifer did. He craved worship, he became obsessed with it. In his newly formed kingdom, he was the dictator: Satan, the cruel dictator of the kingdom of darkness. Of course he had no intention of letting his subjects know that they were under his dictatorship. He would offer a choice of "good and evil". But once they were in his kingdom, nothing they could do would free them from his power.

Satan sniggered at this epitome of deception and watched for an opportunity to put his malevolent plan into action: a mass hijacking operation.And then came the creation of mankind.

How God delighted in the creation of the first two human beings. He made them different from the angels; body, soul and spirit. Being spirit Himself, God communicates with spirit. He gave them a soul with emotions, will and intellect. The soul can choose whether to worship God or not. God didn't make robots. He let them choose. They could stay in His kingdom under His direction or they could choose to leave that kingdom.

Satan squirmed as he watched that perfect creation. He wanted those two human beings desperately. He craved their worship. They had to belong to him.

It was easier than he expected. His chance came in the garden. Disguised as a serpent he convinced Eve that she was missing out on something. He sowed doubt about God's goodness, made her feel hard done by. And she fell for it.

The moment Eve and her husband ate the fruit of the tree of the knowledge of good and evil, they were hijacked into the kingdom of darkness. In that precise moment, they left behind God's kingdom where God had directed them and where, under His direction, they had governed the creation. Instantly, what had united them with God, snapped, and they experienced spiritual death. Spiritual death means separation.

Now that they were separated from God, there was nothing they could do to re-unite with Him. Sin had entered to contaminate all creation. Just one decision that was not directed by God, left man incapable of saving himself. His spirit, now separated from God, was incapable of perceiving the spiritual world, and his relationship with God was broken. Man's soul now took control of him and he became the centre of his world. His mind became clouded by Satan and he lost his God-given brilliant mental capacity.

Satan the dictator, rubbed his hands together with glee. He'd hijacked two human beings and along with them, the whole of creation.

*** *** ***

Years passed. Centuries rolled by. God's plan, already accomplished in the spiritual realm, was soon to be put into action in the natural or physical realm.

Someone who belonged to God's kingdom must come into the kingdom of darkness and offer up his life so that all those who had been born in that kingdom of darkness could be freed. He must come and rescue them because they were totally incapable of rescuing themselves. God's Son, Jesus, was the only one qualified to carry out the huge rescue operation.

*** *** ***

Satan grimaced. Fear clutched at his heart. He listened intently to the conversations and quickly drew his own conclusions. A king born to the Jews? He would not, no he could not, tolerate a rival. He had to act quickly. The human being he used to carry out his clever plan was King Herod.

Herod, compelled by an inner voice, ordered all baby boys under two years old to be killed. But baby Jesus was not among those babies. Satan frowned.

All through Jesus' life on earth, Satan made vicious attempts to hijack Him into his kingdom. He tried by tempting Jesus to obey him. However if Jesus had obeyed and, through obedience, had given allegiance to Satan, He would have immediately been disqualified to carry out the rescue operation.

Satan doubled his efforts to annihilate Jesus. He attempted to throw Him over a cliff. He stirred everyone up against Him. Driven by desperation he played his last card: witchcraft: death by crucifixion. Just as people stick pins into a voodoo doll to cause death, wicked men drove nails into the living body of God's Son Jesus.

Would witchcraft kill Jesus? Would witchcraft be more powerful than the rescuer? His hands and feet were nailed to a cross. Humanly speaking the prospect of survival looked very bleak.

A shout rent the air, a triumphant shout, not the whimper of a dying, defeated person.

"Father, into Your hands I commit my spirit."

Medically speaking, what happened at that moment is not what happens when a person dies. Usually, when one dies, the spirit leaves a dead body. But Jesus' spirit left a living body, not a dead one. Jesus gave up His life.

Witchcraft didn't kill Jesus. He didn't die exhausted, under the weight of the sin of the world. Nor did He die from the multitudinous infirmities He carried. No! He gave up His life voluntarily to rescue the hijacked.

At that moment, all humanity hijacked by Satan centuries before, was FREED!

At that moment, Satan and all the powers of his kingdom of darkness were defeated.

*** *** ***

Satan snarled. There stood Jesus the victor with His hand outstretched. Trembling with rage the defeated foe was obliged to hand over the keys of death and hell. The only resource he had now was his store of lies.

The angels in heaven quivered with emotion. One from that myriad of worshippers had just been dispatched to earth on a mission - to sit at the entrance to the empty grave of the victor.

The earth shook with a violent earthquake. It was a moment of triumph and indicated the arrival of the angel from the spiritual realm into the physical realm.

Jesus' spirit had returned to His Father; His soul had descended to hell where He had snatched the keys of death and hell from the defeated dictator. One thing remained. God was about to raise His body from the grave. It would be an incorruptible body.

Millions of celestial beings held their breath. Excitement rippled through their ranks. For them it was incomprehensible but nonetheless glorious, that historic moment when God with a power that transcended all earthly power, raised His Son Jesus, from the dead.

*** *** ***

Cowering in the shadows, a captive fingered his chains. Born in the kingdom of darkness, he was one of millions of hijacked humanity. Over the years, he had tried various methods of escape: religion;

good works; promises; penitence. Was he doomed to die in captivity? He sighed deeply, and pulling his filthy rags around his shoulders, slumped into a dejected heap on the smelly floor.

Suddenly, something stirred in his spirit compelling him to open his eyes. Instinctively, he knew that his rescuer had come. The risen Jesus stood in front of him with a paper in His hand. Seized with an overwhelming desire to pay attention to what he was being offered, the captive leaned forward and focused on the paper. His name was written in large print. It was his certificate to freedom signed with the very blood of his rescuer.

This was a crucial life-or-death moment. He had to choose. He could believe, and accept his certificate to freedom or continue to exist in captivity. The captive looked up into the face of his rescuer. Their eyes met, and locked. Without hesitation, he believed and grabbed his certificate to freedom.

Clunk. The leg irons fell to the floor.

Clank. The chains on his wrists snapped open.

The freed captive leapt to his feet, his eyes fixed on his rescuer. Grasping the outstretched hand firmly, he stepped confidently into God's kingdom of light.

I'M COMING BACK

A cock crowed somewhere in the early dawn. In his dreams, the fisherman heard it and groaned. Pain poured into his mind, as distorted faces appeared before his eyes. Faces filled with curiosity, mockery and sarcasm.

Once again, the question shrilled in his ear: *You aren't one of his disciples too, are you?* The automatic answer throbbed in his temples: *I am not. I am not. I am not.*

Again the cock crowed and another question forced itself upon him. *Will this be the way I wake up every morning?*

A deep sadness wrapped itself around him. In a cowardly attempt to deny reality, Peter covered his head with his blanket and cried bitterly.

Suddenly loud knocking and shouts filled the house. With an effort, the man hiding under the blanket came back to the present and recognised the woman's voice.

Mary Magdalene! Peter leant forward, tilted his head and listened. "He's not there. The tomb is empty."

Taken aback, the man stumbled to his feet, crossed the room and threw himself out of the door. His friend John appeared from nowhere, and without a word, the two of them set off along the road to the tomb. Adrenalin raced through their bodies and they began to run.

Confusion filled Peter's mind. So many questions and not one answer. He slackened his pace and John moved ahead, reaching the tomb first. He looked in but did not enter. Peter arrived and went straight into the tomb. At first, he saw nothing, but as his eyes adjusted to the semi-darkness, he made out the stone walls and... Peter stood transfixed. His gaze rested on the strips of linen lying there, as well as the burial cloth that had been round Jesus' head. He stared at it, all folded up by itself, separate from the strips of linen.

John came in but Peter hardly noticed him. He made his way outside blinking in the early morning sunshine. *Could it be true? Or did he imagine it?* As he hurried home, his heart thumped in rhythm to the question: *could it be true?* The cloth folded up by itself. He knew the sign. Every Jewish man knew the sign used between a master and his servant.

When a servant set the dinner table for his master, he made sure it was exactly the way the master wanted it. Then discreetly, just out of sight, he would wait until the master had finished eating. He would not dare touch the table until the master had finished. If the master had done eating, he would get up from the table, wipe his fingers and his mouth, clean his beard and then, wadding up the napkin would toss it on to the table. The wadded napkin meant, "I'm done."

But if the master got up from the table, folded his napkin and laid it beside his plate, the servant would not dare touch the table because... Peter blinked back the tears as the truth shone into his heart. The folded napkin meant, "I'm coming back!"

He remembered his Master's words: *"The Son of Man is going to be delivered into the hands of men. They will kill him, and after three days he will rise."*

THE GREY POWDER
An allegory

"This is for you. **It will do the work for you.**"

The landscape gardener watches as the visitor takes a small packet from his pocket. He squints at the writing and listens as the man launches into a detailed explanation of the benefits of the contents. He listens for a long time; he believes every word.

The visitor eventually hands over the packet, along with a small gadget and leaves as mysteriously as he has arrived.

The gardener scratches his head and tries to recall all the information he has received. According to the visitor, this substance has an extraordinary transforming power. **It will do the work for him.** He will not have to do anything, except depend totally on its power. *No, it is too good to be true.*

Carefully he lays the mysterious packet and the detonator on a high shelf in his tool shed. Some day he will experiment.

Shrugging his shoulders, he goes back to the arduous task of building terraces on the steep hillside. Gigantic boulders stud the area and make the work almost impossible. He wishes he had the strength to split them into smaller, more attractive rocks.

Now and again, he thinks about the grey powder and its transforming power, the powder **that will do the work for him.** He is unsure about that bit. Somehow, he feels more satisfied when the perspiration trickles down his face.

There is something gratifying about the way his muscles ache after he has hauled the huge tree trunks back from the forest. He is proud of the blisters and calluses that form on his hands as he tries to make some impression on the lichen covered boulders.

The packet of powder and the detonator wait, covered with dust and cobwebs on the shelf in the tool shed.

The gardener works long hours but the area is far from looking attractive. *Will the landscaped gardens ever be a reality,* he wonders, *a monument to the perseverance of a hard working person?* From time to time, he straightens his aching back and looks across at the boulders on the far hillside. He frowns.

*** *** ***

Winter arrives, bringing depressing rain. The gardener hates to admit to himself that at times he feels exhausted. It is only his pride that spurs him on, as he manoeuvers heavy, sodden logs to build the terraces. *Oh, how those ugly boulders on the far hillside annoy him.*

One day the gardener picks up the detonator. He looks at it inquisitively and his tired eyes light up. Suddenly he chooses to believe in its capacity. He reaches for the packet of powder. Yes, he will **let it do the work for him.**

Thoughtfully, he makes his way to the boulders on the hillside; he remembers the name of the powder. Dynamite. He also recalls the strict instructions he was given. The visitor had emphasised that in order for the operation to be a success, he had to believe and obey.

He believes, although his hands shake a little as he lights the fuse. *Why, he wonders, does he find it so hard to relinquish his own efforts and trust that grey powder?*

His breath comes in short gasps as he runs for shelter. The explosion deafens him.

Minutes later, he peeps out from his hiding place. He blinks involuntarily. Where are those ugly, unresisting boulders? He stands up and his legs tremble as he walks cautiously over to the split rocks. Simply and powerfully, the grey powder **has done the work for him.**

*** *** ***

I've been thinking a lot about dynamite.

The word 'dynamite' comes from the Greek word *'dunamis'* and means *power.* I find it is used dozens of times in the New Testament and refers to the miraculous life-changing power of God.

Paul, in his letter to the Ephesians, shares some amazing information. This power is for us who believe. In the words of the Amplified New Testament: *"So that you can know and understand what is the immeasurable and unlimited and surpassing greatness of His power in and for us who believe, as demonstrated in the working of His mighty strength, which He exerted in Christ when He raised him from the dead..."* (Ephesians 1:19, 20).

It's the 'resurrection dynamite' that is in me.

I have not the slightest doubt that I am a carrier of this divine dynamite. So, if it is there, why don't I see the effect of it in my life? Is it suffocated? Is it damp? I acknowledge that heaps of hay and stacks of stubble are piled on top of it. Like the landscape gardener, I feel more satisfied when I exert my energy, when I collapse exhausted after my efforts. I get pleasure from *doing.* My works suffocate and dampen the divine dynamite.

In order for the divine dynamite in me to manifest its power, I must relinquish my own efforts and use the detonator. Faith. I must believe that the power is there and that simply and powerfully, **He will do the work for me.**

Next time I ride in an elevator, queue in the bank or mingle with the shoppers in the supermarket, I'll whisper this phrase to myself: *"I'm carrying dynamite."* If I do this often enough, I may just begin to believe it and let Christ live His resurrection life in me.

TEARS

Verity eased her bony frame into the rickety old rocking chair and, with an effort, set it moving. The chair seemed as tired as she was, that sultry afternoon.

Physically, the octogenarian wasn't up to much these days but her tiredness went deeper than flesh and bone. Her soul was tired and her emotions frazzled, as she waited for things that never happened.

Her ears were tired of straining to hear her mobile phone ring, but her son never contacted her. Her mind was tired of trying to figure out how to use this latest technology he had given her.

Wearily she looked around. Her eyes rested on her collection of antique miniature vases; she reached out and fingered one twisted into the shape of a trumpet lily. She liked curious things and had taught her children to appreciate them, so it was not surprising that her son, Mark, was out in the Middle East digging holes in the ground.

He wrote fascinating articles. The latest was about the tear bottles that the archaeological team had found in some ancient tomb. Verity had read the article at least five times, because just to read it brought her boy close. She reached for the magazine. In her melancholy frame of mind, the information struck a chord.

These tear bottles were made of thin glass with a slender body, broad at the base, with a funnel-shaped top.

Every member of the family owned a tear bottle and they collected the tears of the whole family. When serious trouble or a death occurred in the home, all the relatives came and each one brought his tear bottle with him. As they wept and wailed, the tears rolling down their cheeks, each person took his or her tear bottle and gathered tears from the faces of all those present.

The bottle was exceedingly important to them. It represented all the heartaches, sorrows and bereavements from the grandparents down to the smallest child. When a person died, his tear bottle was buried with him as one of his most sacred possessions.[3]

---

3   Strange Scriptures that Perplex the Western Mind by Barbara Bowen

The article ended abruptly. *Like death itself,* Verity thought.

She stroked the blurred image of the group of archaeologists. Mark was there, holding a tear bottle.

With a deep sigh, she shut her eyes. A tear spilled over and trickled slowly down a deep wrinkle.

As she dozed, something gently touched her cheek.

Was it He who collects all our tears and preserves them in His bottle? Who else would care about the sorrow of a lonely old woman?

Verity stirred a little, and then fell into a deep sleep.

Later, much later, Verity awoke comforted. Her body felt rested and her soul peaceful, as she sat contentedly rocking in the twilight.

Suddenly her mobile phone shrilled. Verity pressed it to her ear and smiled.

A DRY TREE

The teenager clenched his teeth and his fists in a supreme effort to hide his feelings as he limped across the courtyard. Waves of nausea swept over him.

"It's for your own good." His mother's words hammered in his aching head.

Without anaesthesia, in cold blood, his masculine identity had just disappeared under the humiliating slash of a sharp knife. He clutched at his stomach and retched. Female sniggering came from behind a curtain nearby. Somehow, he straightened up and kept walking towards his living quarters.

"Your position demands it." He recalled the sneer on the official's face during the interview.

It had all sounded so tantalising, a position in the royal palace, status, security. Then the sharp reality: castration. Blinded by the excruciating pain, he all but stumbled on the knotted root of a dry tree. He stopped, leant against the rough trunk and looked up at the dead branches. They reached towards him, taunting him. No leaves, no fruit.

Who am I? What am I? He struggled with his new identity: a eunuch. A groan escaped his lips and his eyes filled with tears he was too proud to let fall.

"That's me. I'm only a dry tree."

*** *** ***

Days turned into weeks and his wound became a scar. Time erased the humiliating memories — all but one. The words crackled like sunburnt twigs. *I'm only a dry tree.*

Elegant robes covered his shame. Gold graced his neck and clinked in his pockets, but deep down inside, the eunuch knew and believed he was a second-class citizen. He was valued only for what he did, not for what he was.

The work was exacting, and demanded all his attention. Promotion followed promotion. Then one day Queen Candace named him Treasurer of Ethiopia.

*** *** ***

The African dignitary stood alone watching the crowds enter the temple. He too had come to Jerusalem to worship, but Jewish law placed a restriction on him. The words of that law cut into his soul as he repeated them under his breath:

"No one who has been emasculated by crushing or cutting may enter the assembly of the Lord." [4]

Anger, resentment and impotence jostled for first place in his mind. *Excluded even by God? Not allowed to worship with His people? Cut off? Had God cut him off? He had no descendants to carry on his name; when he died, his name would just disappear from memory.*

An outcast, ostracised; he felt dozens of eyes boring into him. He lowered his head. *He was a foreigner, a eunuch, a dry tree. Why ever had he come?*

---

4   Deuteronomy 23:1

*** *** ***

The Treasurer settled himself into his carriage and reached for the scroll. The journey from Jerusalem back to Ethiopia was tedious and reading aloud would help pass the time.

"He was led like a lamb to the slaughter, and as a sheep before its shearers is silent, so he did not open his mouth." [5]

The Treasurer scratched his head. *Who did this refer to?*

"By oppression and judgment he was taken away. And who can speak of his descendants? For he was cut off from the land of the living..." [6]

Cut off? Without descendants? Who was the prophet talking about? Suddenly, he was aware of a man walking beside his chariot. *How odd,* he thought. *There was no one there a minute ago.*

"Do you understand what you are reading?"

The Treasurer frowned.

"How can I, unless someone explains it to me? Come up and sit with me."

The African stretched out his hand and welcomed the stranger who introduced himself as Philip.

"Tell me please, who is the prophet talking about, himself or someone else?"

Philip took the scroll in his hands and began reading Isaiah's prophecy, explaining how it talked about Jesus. The eunuch leant forward and soaked up every word. The message of Jesus touched his withered spirit. *Oppressed, afflicted, judged, taken away, cut off.* He identified with Jesus.

"After the suffering of his soul, he will see the light of life and be satisfied." [7]

The water of life seeped into the dry barren ground of the man's soul. He sighed deeply. He couldn't remember ever having felt truly satisfied.

---

5   Isaiah 53
6   Ibid
7   Ibid

"He will bear their iniquities… He made intercession for the transgressors." [8]

The eunuch lowered his head. He was a transgressor, a lawbreaker. The chariot kept moving. The eunuch kept listening and believing. In a curious way, he felt revitalised emotionally and spiritually, and yes, physically, almost as if warm sap was running through his veins. As they travelled along, they came to some water.

"Look, here is water. What can stand in the way of my being baptised?"

The eunuch held his breath. *Would there be an obstacle? Would this be another desire denied him as a consequence of his sexual situation? Another "No"?*

"If you believe with all your heart, you may."

"I believe that Jesus Christ is the Son of God." He spoke with confidence and, without hesitation, ordered the carriage to come to a halt.

He climbed down. Philip followed and together they went down into the water. The eunuch closed his eyes as the water washed over his head. When he opened them, Philip was nowhere to be seen.

Mystified, he climbed back into the carriage and immediately reached for the scroll, thirsty to read more. Not in his wildest dreams did he imagine how the words he was about to read would change his life.

*** *** ***

"Let no foreigner who has bound himself to the Lord say, The Lord will surely exclude me from his people. And let not any eunuch complain, I am only a dry tree." [9]

The eunuch gasped.

He re-read the last phrase: *"And let not any eunuch complain, I am only a dry tree."*

---

8   Ibid
9   Isaiah 56

A scene flashed before his eyes. He saw himself, a mutilated humiliated teenager. He felt the physical agony, the emotional torment, the spiritual significance and heard for the last time the taunting refrain: *Only a dry tree.*

He swallowed and continued reading: *"For this is what the Lord says: To the eunuchs who keep my Sabbaths, who choose what pleases me and hold fast to my covenant— to them I will give within my temple and its walls a memorial and a name better than sons and daughters; I will give them an everlasting name that will not be cut off."* [10]

He blinked back the tears. Another scene came before him: a man outside the temple, his head bowed in shameful acceptance that he was a foreigner, a eunuch. Wiping his eyes, he continued reading: *"And foreigners who bind themselves to the Lord to serve him, to love the name of the Lord, and to worship him, all who keep the Sabbath without desecrating it and who hold fast to my covenant—these I will bring to my holy mountain and give them joy in my house of prayer. Their burnt offerings and sacrifices will be accepted on my altar; for my house will be called a house of prayer for all nations."* [11]

Running his finger under the vital words, he re-read them aloud: *"foreigners... I will bring to my holy mountain... give them joy in my house of prayer... their burnt offerings and sacrifices will be accepted on my altar..."*

Accepted!

Satisfied, the eunuch leaned back in his carriage, closed his eyes and smiled. Waves of joy swept over him.

---

10   Ibid
11   Ibid

A MIRACLE FOR MATIAS
A story for children

Matias is a handsome grey rabbit with soft fur and long floppy ears. He lives in a comfortable rabbit hutch with a white rabbit called Snowball. Every day Natalie gives them rabbit food to eat and clean water to drink.

This is the true story of how Matias received a miracle.

One day Natalie noticed that Matias didn't eat his breakfast. He didn't eat his lunch either. Natalie lifted him out of the rabbit hutch to have a good look at him. She discovered a nasty lump under his little furry chin. Very carefully, Natalie opened his tiny mouth and saw why he didn't want to eat. He couldn't eat, because one tooth was only half the size it should be.

Natalie and her friend, Joey, decided to take Matias to the vet. He would know what to do about the nasty lump and the half size tooth. But the vet said, "I don't treat rabbits at my clinic."

Natalie took the sick rabbit in her arms, and she and Joey walked out of the clinic door. They were very sad and Natalie started to cry. They decided to go to another vet who had an animal hospital in the city. They walked and walked until they got to the animal hospital. The vet examined Matias very carefully. He poked the nasty lump and frowned. He saw the half-sized tooth and slowly shook his head. Then he talked to Joey and Natalie.

"This rabbit is very sick," he told them. "There is nothing I can do. The lump will grow bigger. Even if I give him medicine, he will die because he is not able to eat. The lump is making his teeth break in pieces."

That was sad, bad news. The vet charged them a lot of money for examining Matias. Joey took his precious savings out of his trouser pocket and handed the money to the vet. Then they walked out on to the street, feeling very sad indeed.

"Let's go and see my mum," suggested Joey.

All the way to Joey's house, Natalie cuddled Matias in her arms. The two children did not talk because they were thinking about what the vet had told them. Joey's mother listened to the sad, bad news.

"Let's ask God to heal Matias," she said.

She sat down and took Matias on her knee. Joey brought her some oil and she put a little on the nasty lump. Natalie and Joey listened carefully while she talked to God.

This is what she said: "Dear God, Matias is Your creation. He was created to bring glory to You. As Matias is Your creation, I command the cells in his body to obey their Creator."

She gently stroked Matias' soft grey head and handed him back to Natalie.

Ten days later Natalie noticed that Matias was eating his breakfast. She lifted him out of his hutch and put her fingers under his furry chin. The nasty lump had gone! She carefully opened his tiny mouth and guess what she saw? Matias had a new tooth! Matias had received a miracle from God.

Every day Matias grew fatter. He was not a sick rabbit anymore. Joey and Natalie said a big "Thank you" to God for making Matias better.

And the end of this true story? Matias and Snowball now have two beautiful baby bunnies.

SET FREE TO SERVE

God is not unrighteous to forget your… labour of love.

Hebrews 10:6

A TRIBUTE TO ALL PARENTS OF MISSIONARIES

God is not unrighteous to forget your… labour of love. Hebrews 10:6

Labour of love?
You say, "What have we done?"
– Seeking not the limelight,
Seeking not men's praise –
Eternity alone will tell
All you have done.

Two daughters were born to you,
And all unselfishly
You gave them back to Him.
To His service, you dedicated them;
God took you at your word,
He led them far away
And all unselfishly you let them go.

Conscious of your deep, deep love,
Aware of constant prayer,

Grateful for your great unselfishness,
We revel in the freedom you have given us:
    Freedom to serve the Lord to whom you dedicated us:
    Freedom to share the love we have received,
    Freedom to give because you gave,
    Freedom to do all He asks us to do,
    Freedom to be all He asks us to be.

SET FREE TO SERVE

The temporal would bind my spirit.
Free me Lord,
To live above the things of time.
Teach me Lord.
All I have, Master, is Yours,
I lay it on my open palm.
From all I have and hold,
Free me, Lord.

A heart at leisure from itself,
Grant me, Lord.
To love and live from self set free,
Teach me Lord.
To find the rest that's found in You,
To see, reach out and learn to care,
The "I" all insignificant,
Grant me, Lord.

A SHEPHERD WHO SMELLS OF SHEEP

Lord, I want to be a shepherd who smells of sheep;
A paramedic whose hands are smeared with blood and dirt;
An intercessor with tears on my cheeks.

Lord, teach me to look, in order to **see**.
Look behind the flawless makeup and the forced smile,
To detect the fear reflected in those eyes;
See the anguish behind the scowl and frown.

Lord, teach me to listen, so that I may **hear**;
Hear the sob disguised in harsh words,
Capture the message masked by fast, brittle talk.
Hear the wail from a wounded heart;
Hear the desperate cry for help;
Hear what they longed to say, but didn't.

Lord, teach me to sense, so I can **feel**.
Sense the unspoken need,
Perceive the void in the life of my brother,
Perceive the emotional pain my sister is suffering.
Feel with compassion, and love with your love.

Lord, teach me to intercede.
(Not to have a list of people for whom I pray,
but to pray for people).
Intercede with compassion and tears,
for people with needs and unspoken fears;
for the rich who really have nothing;
for the self-sufficient who lack everything.

Lord, make me a shepherd who smells of sheep;
A paramedic whose hands are smeared with blood and dirt;
An intercessor with tears on my cheeks.

REACH OUT

Reach out. You'll never regret it.
Reach out. There's joy in store.
Reach out. You'll find it's worth it.
Reach out. Give someone time today.

Reach out. You'll find you like it.
Reach out. You'll be glad you did.
Reach out. You'll keep on doing it.
Reach out. Touch a life today.

Reach out. You'll receive a blessing.
Reach out. Dare to get involved.
Reach out. You'll find it a challenge.
Reach out. Help a soul today.

Reach out. Feel that inner warmness.
Reach out. You'll find you're blessed.
Reach out. There's someone waiting.
Reach out. Lend a hand today.

Reach out. You could start a friendship.
Reach out. You may win a soul.
Reach out. Your life will be richer.
Reach out. Why not start today?

Reach out. You'll find you like it.
Reach out. You'll be glad you did.
Reach out. You'll keep on doing it.
Reach out. Touch a life today.

IT'S ALL ABOUT HIM

For I resolved to know nothing while I was with you
except Jesus Christ and Him crucified.

1 Corinthians 2:2

NO BLACK SQUIGGLES

Minnie's eyes clouded over.

She could make neither head nor tail of the black squiggles on the white board. And she didn't want to. She sat through the remainder of the discipleship class completely detached.

I was sitting in on the class and saw when we lost her. I knew why. Minnie was illiterate.

The information written on the whiteboard was life-changing. We couldn't leave her stumbling along the path of religion, trying to earn what had already been paid for.

By the following Sunday morning class, I had the answer. There were no black squiggles to squint at, or to ignore. There were pictures.

Minnie's eyes lit up.

*** *** ***

These simple pictures are powerful. The absence of written words provokes animated discussion in small groups.

What does the cloud represent?

Who are the three little fellows? Why three and not four, or two?

Why is the tall fellow in the second picture so happy?

Folk express ideas and come to conclusions. They discover the cloud is a Who, not a what. They give names to the little fellows, and scribble key words as they grasp the good news, the gospel.

This presentation gives nominal Christians the opportunity to be born again. Good people realise it's not about being good.

P.S. Author's note: The following diagram has no copyright. The more copies made the better.

GUIDE TO DIAGRAM

How to use this evangelism tool.

When God created the first human beings, He created them with a perfect design.

A human being is a spiritual being who has a soul and lives in a body.

God gave him a **spirit** so that he could communicate with Him because God is a spirit.

God gave him a **soul** (emotions, intellect and will). The soul is the bridge between the spirit and the body; it is a de-coder that transmits the spiritual to the natural.

The **body** is the outer case, which permits the human being to live in the natural world. God gave this human being free will, the capacity to obey Him or choose to live independently from Him as a result of disobeying Him.

What happened to the original design?

When Adam and Eve sinned by eating from the tree of the Knowledge of Good and Evil, they chose to become independent from God. Immediately the communication between God and the human race was cut off.

The spirit dies because separation from God is spiritual death.

The soul gets bigger and starts to exert its own will; it does right and wrong things according to its own criteria. But it doesn't realise it is just a marionette in Satan's hands. There is now nothing that it can do by itself, to restore the communication with God. (The soul was kidnapped and taken away to the kingdom of darkness, to Satan's territory).

Because of this situation and this condition, this person is a sinner.

Everyone born on this earth is in this condition. I was born a sinner, separated from God. You were born like that too, a sinner, separated from God.

How can we re-connect with God?

What do you need, in order to change your condition as a sinner?

Who can re-connect you with God

Who can rescue you from the kidnapper?

A saviour!

The Saviour's name is Jesus Christ.

When Jesus died on the cross, He defeated Satan and paid the rescue price. He is the only one who can re-connect you with God.

Would you like to tell Him that you recognise your condition as a sinner? That you believe that He died to save you, and that He paid the rescue price?

"Lord Jesus Christ, I recognise that I was born separated from God, in the condition of a sinner. I realise that in this condition, I cannot do anything to re-connect with God. I need a saviour. I believe with all my heart that You are the One who paid the price to rescue me when You died on the cross. Thank You for saving me, for rescuing me and for relocating me in Your kingdom. I accept You as my Saviour; I accept Your government and decide to leave the kingdom of darkness where I was born. Today I am born into Your kingdom. I decide to live under Your direction."

GOD'S TRUTH VERSUS HUMAN TRUTH

We are spiritual beings. Although we usually say body, soul and spirit, the order is incorrect. We are spirit, we have a soul and we live in a body.

God is spirit. He communicates with man's spirit, not with man's soul. Our soul is our emotions, intellect and will. Therefore, if we try to communicate with God with our soul, we don't get the answers we long for. We plead for what we want, what we think is best, all based on what we see and experience. We are praying with our soul and as we have seen in the diagram, God doesn't communicate with our soul, but with our spirit. Our 'soul prayers' just go up as far as the ceiling.

Hebrews 4:12 reads: *"For the word of God is alive and active. Sharper than any double-edged sword, it penetrates even to dividing soul and spirit, joints and marrow; it judges the thoughts and attitudes of the heart."*

Is there something that can separate my soul from my spirit enabling me to pray with my spirit? Yes. It is a sword; it is the Word of God.

So, I won't talk to God about what I see around me, what I hear with my natural ears, what I want, what I think is best. God's Word penetrates and separates my soul, putting it quietly aside. God's Word will enable me to move to a deeper level, where I no longer adjust my thinking to human truth, but begin to believe God's truth.

There is an enormous difference between **human truth and God's truth.** As we learn to declare God's truth over our particular situation, the intense light of the Word of God shines into the darkness and reveals the lies we have believed. If we are lonely, we discover that we are never alone, because God's Word says He will never leave us. If we suffer from depression, we find that God's Word gives us the words to express our feelings to God. We can admit that though we sit in darkness the Lord will be our light; that we need not be dismayed because He is our God. When we feel unloved, insecure and rejected we can learn to pray God's truth and discover that His love is unfailing, He loves unconditionally, and even if, for example, our parents have rejected us (human truth, because it really did happen), the Lord receives us. It is what God says about the situation that counts. What He says, is what it is.

It is not what we think about ourselves, but what God's Word says about us; it is not what we feel about ourselves, but what God's Word declares we are; it is not what we see with our human eyes but what God's Word shows us. It really is ALL ABOUT HIM.

Each time we are heavy hearted or distressed because of a situation or because we have believed a lie of Satan, we can declare aloud **GOD'S TRUTH.**

GOD'S TRUTH, MY IDENTITY IN CHRIST

Thank You Lord, for the right to be Your child. I confess that I am a child of God, because I have received You and have believed in Your name (John 1:12).

Lord, I confess with my mouth that Jesus is Lord. I believe in my heart that God raised Jesus from the dead. I testify that I am saved. I am justified because I have believed in my heart, and saved because I confess with my mouth (Romans 10:9).

Lord, my body is Your temple because the Holy Spirit lives in me. You bought me with the highest price in the universe – Your precious blood. Teach me to honour You with my body (1 Corinthians 6:19-20).

Thank You Lord, that you chose me before the creation of the world to be holy and blameless in Your sight. Thank You that it is Your blood that makes me holy. I declare that I am holy (Ephesians 1:4).

Thank You Lord for rescuing me from the dominion of darkness. I declare that Satan has no power over me. I belong to the kingdom of Jesus Christ for ever (Colossians 1:13).

Thank You Lord that You came to destroy the works of the devil. I proclaim that all the works of the devil in my life are destroyed (1 John 3:8).

Thank You God for forgiving all my sins, and for cancelling the written code that was against me (Colossians 2:13, 14). You have justified me and there is nobody who can condemn me (Romans 8: 33).

Lord I take the victory that I have been given through the Lord Jesus Christ (1 Corinthians 15:57). I am more than a conqueror (Romans 8:37).

Lord, I know the truth and that truth sets me free (John 8:32). I will stand firm in this freedom and I will not be burdened by a yoke of slavery (Galatians 5:1).

Lord, I testify that I am in Christ, and that I am a new creature. I renounce all that has passed and declare that in Christ all things are new (2 Corinthians 5:17).

Lord, thank You for the powerful weapons that You have given me. In the name of the Lord Jesus I take captive every thought to make it obedient to Christ, in order to demolish all the enemy's strongholds (2 Corinthians 10:3-5).

I proclaim that I have the mind of Christ (1 Corinthians 2:16).

PROCLAIM GOD'S TRUTH FOR OTHERS

Lord, I thank You for giving _____ the power to be Your child. He/she is a child of God, because he/she has received You and has believed in Your name (John 1:12).

Lord, I declare that _____ confesses with his/her mouth that Jesus Christ is Lord. He/she believes in his/her heart that God raised Jesus Christ from the dead. I testify that he/she is saved; he/she is justified because he/she has believed in his/her heart, and saved because he/she confesses this with his/her mouth (Romans 10:9-10).

Lord, I declare that _____ is Your temple because the Holy Spirit lives in him/her. You bought him/her with the highest price in the universe – Your precious blood. Teach him/her to glorify You in his/her body (1 Corinthians 6:19-20).

Thank You Lord that You chose _____ to be holy, since before You created the world. Thank You that your blood makes him/her holy. I declare that he/she is holy (Ephesians 1:4).

Thank You Lord, for delivering _____ from the power of darkness. I announce that Satan has no power over him/her. He/she belongs to the kingdom of Jesus Christ forever (Colossians 1:13).

Thank You Lord that you came to undo the works of the devil in _____'s life. I proclaim that all the works of Satan in his/her life are undone (1 John 3:8).

Thank God for forgiving all _____'s sins and for cancelling the written code against him/her (Colossians 2:13-14). You have justified him/her and no one can accuse him/her of anything (Romans 8:33).

Lord, _____ takes for himself/herself the victory that is his/hers in Christ Jesus. Yes! He/she has the victory through Jesus Christ. (1 Corinthians 15:57). He/she is more than a conqueror (Romans 8:37).

Lord, _____knows the truth and that truth makes him/her free. (John 8:32). He/she will be firm in that freedom and will not be slave to anything (Galatians 5:1).

Lord, I testify that _____is in Christ, and that he/she is a new creature. He/she renounces all the past and announces that all things in Christ are new (2 Corinthians 5:17).

Lord, thank You for the powerful weapons that You have given _____. In the name of Jesus Christ, he/she takes captive every thought to the obedience of Christ, in order to destroy the enemy's strongholds (2 Corinthians 10:3-5). I proclaim that he/she has the mind of Christ (1 Corinthians 2:16).

IT'S ALL BEEN DONE

God created time, space and matter and they are subject to Him.

God the great I AM, lives and moves in an eternal present, outside of the restrictions of time. Therefore, **time** is not an impediment to God to fulfil in the natural world what He has already done in the spiritual world.

Space as part of God's creation is subject to Him. Space does not restrict His power; nor does distance diminish it.

Matter does not obstruct or hinder God's power. As His creation, it submits to Him.

Revelation 13:8 shows that the Lamb was slain from the foundation of the world. By His words **"It is finished"** Jesus Christ announced that everything was finished. His work was completed; it transcends, that is, it goes beyond time, and cuts across space.

How is Christ's finished work on the cross of benefit to me in the 21st century?

The blood that Jesus Christ shed on the cross is **valid** today; it has no 'use by' date. It **washed** away my sin, **cleansed** me of its contamination and **removed** my iniquity.

Through Christ's work on the cross, I was **rescued** from Satan's dominion and **relocated** in the Kingdom of God.

What Jesus Christ did **in me and for me** on the cross will never lose its power to **transform**, **heal** and **bless** me.

Through the following verses of Scripture, I declare that **the power of Christ's work on the cross remains valid, and is present in my life today.**

"When he had received the drink, Jesus said, 'It is finished'. With that, he bowed his head and gave up his spirit" (John 19:30). Thank You Lord Jesus for those words, "It is finished". I declare that on the cross, You completed what you came to earth to do. I put my faith in what you have already done, because everything, absolutely everything You came to do, is finished.

"The lamb that was slain from the foundation of the world" (Revelation 13:8). Heavenly Father thank You that when Adam and Eve sinned, You didn't have to revert to a Plan B. In the spiritual realm, the Lamb had already been slain. From the creation of the world, Your plan to rescue, redeem, forgive, heal and bless me had already been carried out. Jesus completed His work on the cross. I believe in His finished work, I accept it and acknowledge Him as my Rescuer, Redeemer, Saviour, Healer, and the One who forgave me and blessed me with every spiritual blessing.

"Surely he took up our pain and bore our suffering, yet we considered him punished by God, stricken by him, and afflicted. But he was pierced for our transgressions, he was crushed for our iniquities; the punishment that brought us peace was on him, and by his wounds we are healed" (Isaiah 53:4-5). I believe that You,

Jesus Christ, took up my pain and bore my suffering. Your Word says it, so I believe it. Your Father punished You instead of me. You were afflicted, pierced for my transgressions, crushed for my iniquities. The punishment that brought me peace was on You. I am healed by Your wounds. The words "Thank you" seem so inadequate to express my gratitude. You took what I deserved, and gave me what I didn't deserve.

"God made him who had no sin to be sin for us, so that in him we might become the righteousness of God" (2 Corinthians 5:21). My dear Lord Jesus, I am amazed that God made You, who had no sin, to be sin for me. You became sin, so that in You I could become the righteousness of God. My sin, Your righteousness. What an incredible exchange. I declare that I am righteous in You.

"God demonstrates his own love for us in this: while we were still sinners, Christ died for us" (Romans 5:8). I recognise that because I was born a sinner, I deserved death. Lord Jesus, You took my place on the cross. Thank You for dying so that I might have life – another amazing exchange: death for You, life for me. What a demonstration of Your love, Father God. I receive that life.

"Christ redeemed us from the curse of the law by becoming a curse for us, for it is written: 'Cursed is everyone who is hanged on a tree'" (Galatians 3:13). How could it be, dear Lord Jesus, that You became a curse for me? You redeemed me from the curse of the law and for me there is only blessing. Thank You! I declare I have every spiritual blessing in Christ.

"You know the grace of our Lord Jesus Christ, that though he was rich, yet for your sake he became poor, so that you through his poverty might become rich" (2 Corinthians 8:9). Lord Jesus, You became poor so that I might become rich. You emptied yourself and poured all your riches into me. Through Your poverty, I am blessed with every spiritual blessing.

"For we know that our old self was crucified with him so that the body ruled by sin might be rendered powerless, that we should

no longer be slaves to sin. In the same way, count yourselves dead to sin but alive to God in Christ Jesus" (Romans 6:6,11). I decide to believe that my old self was crucified with You, Lord Jesus on the cross. The body ruled by sin was rendered powerless. I decide that I will no longer be a slave to sin. I choose to count myself dead to sin, and alive to God, in You, Christ Jesus. You are my life. You live Your life in me.

"Therefore, since we have been justified through faith, we have peace with God through our Lord Jesus Christ, through whom we have gained access by faith into this grace in which we now stand" (Romans 5:1-2). I declare I have been justified through faith. I have peace with You, Heavenly Father through Jesus Christ. Through Him I have gained access into this grace in which I now stand. Your grace, the mercy I didn't deserve, amazes me. I will never cease to praise You for what You did *for* me and *in* me on the cross!

"Faith is confidence in what we hope for and assurance about what we do not see" (Hebrews 11:1). Thank You Heavenly Father that You are not limited by time, space or material things. I believe that the spiritual world, although invisible, is permanent and eternal. I do not see it, but I have the assurance it is real. I declare that all that Jesus did for me and in me on the cross is valid today. I praise You Father, that Christ's work on the cross has no *'use by'* date. I find the solution for all the situations in my life, in the finished work of Jesus Christ on the cross.

FAITH'S ENEMIES

Faith has two enemies: unbelief and human reasoning.

Unbelief has become the means by which we assess reality; we decide what is possible and what we deem impossible.

Reason does not allow us to believe God; it puts us in a prison that limits His power, where we eat from the tree of the knowledge of good and evil, and where we don't need faith.

Faith goes beyond human reason. Faith comes first, followed by understanding.

Our faith must be renewed on a daily basis; yesterday's faith isn't faith today!

I choose to exercise my faith as I pray through the following Scripture verses:

Have faith in God (Mark 11:22). Heavenly Father, I confess that my human nature is not capable of having faith because it always looks for reason and logic. I acknowledge that reason and logic are faith's worst enemies; they make me doubt. I decide to exercise faith in God and believe that He is who He says He is; He did what He says He has done; I am what He says I am. I praise You Lord, because I participate in the divine nature, and that nature believes and cannot doubt.

"Against all hope, Abraham in hope believed... without weakening in his faith... he did not waver through unbelief regarding the promise of God, but was strengthened in his faith and gave glory to God, being fully persuaded that God had power to do what he had promised. This is why 'it was credited to him as righteousness'" (Romans 4:17-22). Lord, today I choose to believe in hope against hope because I know in whom I believe. I open up my heart and allow You to destroy all doubt, disbelief, reasoning and argument with the dynamite of Your faith. I strengthen myself in Your faith and give You all the glory. I am convinced that You are able to do what You have promised. I declare that Your faith in me is counted for righteousness. I declare that in Christ, I am righteous.

"See to it, brothers and sisters, that none of you has a sinful, unbelieving heart that turns away from the living God" (Hebrews 3:12). Lord, I confess the unbelief in my heart and renounce my tendency to assess my situation by what I myself decide is possible and what seems impossible. I recognise that the failures in my life are the result of my own disbelief. I decide to use the measure of faith I have and put it into practice in my current situation.

By faith we understand (Hebrews 11:3). Heavenly Father, I acknowledge that many times when I do not understand You, I do not believe You. Your Word teaches me that faith must be first, then understanding. I refuse to allow Satan to imprison me within the limits of reason. I renounce trying to understand You, using reason. I declare that faith does not need human reason to believe, because faith surpasses all reason and is not based on common sense. I decide to align my thoughts with Your thoughts in order to increase my level of faith.

"For therein is the righteousness of God revealed from faith to faith; as it is written: 'The just shall live by faith'" (Romans 1:17). Lord I declare that Your righteousness is not only revealed by faith, but also in order to increase my faith. Teach me to exercise my faith and take the first step so that You can show me the next step. I am attentive to what You want to do in my life; I put my hand in Yours and decide to live by faith.

DIGGING TREASURES FROM EPHESIANS CHAPTER 1

I praise and thank You Father God for all the blessings I have in Christ Jesus. You have already blessed me in the heavenly realm in Christ. I declare that I am in Christ, I belong to Him and therefore all the spiritual blessings are mine (Ephesians 1:3).

Lord, I marvel that You chose me in Christ before the creation of the world. You chose me to be holy and blameless in Your sight. You see me as holy, because I am in Christ (Ephesians 1:4).

Lord, You not only chose me, but it was always in Your mind to adopt me as Your own child. Thank You for adopting me into Your family through Jesus Christ. Thank You God, that I can call You Father (Ephesians 1:5).

I praise You Father God for Your wonderful kindness, for the grace and favour You pour out on me. You accept me because I belong to Jesus Christ, the Son You love so dearly (Ephesians 1:6).

Your love for me is so great, that You redeemed me through the blood of Your Son, Jesus Christ. You bought my freedom. You forgave me. I praise You and bless you. I am redeemed! I am forgiven (Ephesians 1:7).

Thank You Father God for the richness of Your grace that You shower down on me. You understand me and in your great wisdom, You know what is the best for me. Thank You for sending Jesus Your Son to fulfil Your plan. What You propose, You carry through. You bring together all things in heaven and on earth under one head, Jesus Christ (Ephesians 1:8-10).

Thank You God my Father for the inheritance that is mine because I am in Christ. You chose me to be Yours from the very beginning. Everything happens in accordance to Your plan. I put my hope in Christ and declare that I exist for the praise of Your glory (Ephesians 1:11-12).

CHARISMA OR CHRIST'S CHARACTER

Thank You Father God, for Your Holy Spirit who lives in me; He develops Your character in me. You have placed in me the incorruptible Seed, the anointed Christ Himself. Heavenly Father, I renounce my own personal image, in order for You to develop and make visible the image of Christ in me (Gal 5:22, 23). I accept the fact that I can only produce the fruit of the flesh, so I choose to cultivate the Seed and allow You to produce the Spirit's fruit in my life. I decide to let Christ live His life in me (Galatians 2:20).

My thought life reveals my true character

Father God, Your Word teaches me that what I think, I am (Proverbs 23:7). Today I decide to think about what is true, noble, just and pure; I choose to think about lovely, good and commendable things and to meditate on things worthy of praise (Phil 4:8). I take captive every thought to the obedience of Christ (2 Corinthians 10:5), and declare that I have the mind of Christ (1 Corinthians 2:16).

What I most value reveals my character

Lord, I acknowledge that my heart is with what I most value (Matthew 6:21). I choose to give You the first place, the pre-eminence in all the areas of my life. Fill me Lord, with the Water of Life, so that I will never be thirsty for the transient things of this world (John 4:13-14).

My motives reveal my true character

You my Heavenly Father, search the minds and hearts (Revelation 2:23). My motives are more important to You than my actions. I can deceive those around me, but You know me. Teach me Lord, to act motivated by Your Spirit, and alert me when my motives are incorrect.

My feelings reveal my true character

Lord I declare that Your love has been shed abroad in my heart by Your Holy Spirit that You have given me (Romans 5:5). I acknowledge that my love is limited, carnal and conditional. I receive Your love that is without limits, heavenly and unconditional. Teach me to love others with Your love.

My actions reveal my true character

Lord, I understand that my actions are the result of my thoughts, of what I value, of what motivates me and how I feel. I renounce lending my body to the devil in order to act in the flesh and decide to do everything to bring glory to God (1 Corinthians 10:31). Thank You Lord, that the good work You have begun in me, You promise to complete (Phil 1:6). Thank You for developing Your character in me. **Charisma is temporal but Your character in me is eternal.**

I REST IN YOUR SOVEREIGNTY

Thank You heavenly Father that I am not here by chance. Before the world ever existed, I existed in Your mind (Ephesians 1:4), and Your plan was to form the image of Your Son in me. Your purpose for me is that I am conformed to the image of Christ. I declare that all that happens to me, You use in my favour to achieve Your purpose. I realise the enemy tries to thwart Your purpose and alter my destiny, but I decide to believe that You work everything out in conformity with the purpose of Your will (Ephesians 1:11).

My Father God, Your will is perfect (Romans 12:2). I believe that the work You have begun in me, You will carry on to completion (Philippians 1:6). You have already seen the end of the process. I decide to submit myself to the purpose and plan of Your will because my greatest desire is to be for the praise of Your glory (Ephesians 1: 11, 12).

Lord Jesus, I thank You for Your example. You always did Your Father's will, while You lived on the earth. You never once did Your own will (John 5:30).

Lord, You are the only One whose will is free. I choose to stay united to You, so that my will may be free. I submit to Your free will, in order to carry out Your will for me. I want to always do what You have planned for me. I declare that I am in Christ and I submit to Him, so that His sovereign will is accomplished in my life.

Lord God, I declare myself truly free in Your Son (John 8:36). I make the decision to accept Your will for my life because You are the only One who is free. I line up my desires with Your perfect will for my life and choose to look at things from Your view point. It is You in me, who works in me to will and to act in order to fulfil Your good purpose (Philippians 2:13).

Heavenly Father, I confess that I have put my plans above Yours. I recognise that the only way to be truly happy is to renounce my plans for my life and line up with Yours. I choose to believe that Your plans for me are to prosper me and not to harm me; they are plans to give me hope and a future (Jeremiah 29:11). I ask You to carry out Your plans and purpose in my life.

Lord, I understand that in the beginning Adam and Eve enjoyed 100% free will. When they chose to become independent from You they lost the freedom of their will and were reduced to the choice between good and evil. I praise You Lord because You freed me from the tree of the knowledge of good and evil.

You are the Tree of Life! I choose not only to walk with Christ, but also to live in Him, and in that way recover my free will (1 Corinthians 15:22).

Sovereign God I decide to believe that everything that happens to me, You work for my good, because I have been called according to Your purpose (Romans 8:28, 29). Your purpose is to form the image of Christ in me. I accept that You work through all kinds of people and circumstances in order that Your perfect will becomes a reality in my life. Everything that happens to me is under Your loving control. Truly, You are **sovereign** and I rest in Your sovereignty.

LIFE-CHANGING STATEMENTS

"I was crucified with Christ. With my spiritual eyes, I see myself crucified. I no longer live, but Christ lives in me. I count myself dead to sin but alive to God in Christ Jesus" (Galatians 2:20, Romans 6:11).

"My body of sin was destroyed when I was crucified with Christ. I am no longer a slave to sin. The life I live in the flesh, I live by the faith of the Son of God. I choose to allow Christ to live His life in me and through me" (Romans 6:6, Galatians 2:20).

"Sin no longer reigns in my mortal body; I am not obliged to sin. I choose to offer myself daily to God and declare that the members of my body are instruments of righteousness. I consecrate myself to God" (Romans 6:12-14).

"I am not a slave to sin. I was freed from the law of sin and I am a slave to righteousness. I consecrate myself as a slave to righteousness" (Romans 6:17-18).

"I am in Christ Jesus and there is no condemnation for me. I decide not to walk according to the flesh, but according to the Spirit. I choose to allow Christ to live His life in me and produce the fruit of the Spirit. I declare myself free from *"I must do"* and enjoy the truth that, *'He has already done'"* (Romans 8:1, Galatians 2:20, John 15: 4-5).

"I am free from the law of sin and death because Christ lives in me. The law of the Spirit of life in Him has delivered me. I declare that I am free in Christ Jesus" (Romans 8:2).

"I choose to think about the things of the Spirit because to dwell on the things of the flesh is death. I choose to allow the Holy Spirit to control my mind and as a result I receive life and peace. I choose to live by the Spirit, and in so doing, please God. I declare that I have the Spirit of Christ and that I am His" (Romans 8:6-9).

"Christ is the image of the invisible God. I acknowledge that because of sin, Christ's image in me was ruined, but that through the work of Christ on the cross, it is restored. I submit myself to God and decide to allow Him to form the image of His Son, Jesus Christ, in my life" (Colossians 1:15).

"I affirm that my old self was crucified; I consider myself dead to sin and alive to God in Christ. I present myself to God and declare that the members of my body belong to Him. I choose to walk in the Spirit and submit my soul to God's authority. I affirm that Jesus Christ is my Lord" (Romans 6-8).

GLORY

"For all have sinned and fall short of the glory of God" (Romans 3:23). Heavenly Father, I recognise that I was born deprived of Your glory. Thank You for sending Your Son so that through His death I could regain the image that Adam lost. I declare that I have Christ's image in me, the image of the invisible God. Christ in me, the hope of glory (Colossians 1:27).

"All people are like grass, and all **their glory** is like the flowers of the field; the grass withers and the flowers fall" (1 Peter 1:24). Lord God, I renounce my glory, the glory of humanity that is like grass that withers and flowers that fall. I choose not to glory in my earthly wisdom, nor in my physical strength, nor in my possessions but in knowing You personally and in a practical way (Jeremiah 9:23-24).

"I have given them **the glory that you gave me**, that they may be one as we are one—I in them and you in me—so that they may be brought to complete unity. Then the world will know that you sent me and have loved them even as you have loved me" (John 17:22-23). Lord Jesus, it is wonderful to read what You said to Your Father about the glory that He gave You, and even more wonderful to know that the glory He gave You, You have given to me to unite me, along with You, to Him. Thank You for uniting me with Your Father, and for including me in that union. The Father in You; and You, Lord Jesus, in me. We are one.

"For the earth will be filled with **the knowledge of the glory of the Lord** as the waters cover the sea" (Habakkuk 2:14). Lord Jesus Christ, You are in me and I am in You. You have given me Your glory. I decide to let all those around me see Your glory in me. I will let You speak for me; I will let You look through my eyes. When people look at me, they won't see me, but Your glory that shines through me. I am an ambassador of Your glory on the earth, so that all the earth will be filled with the knowledge of Your glory.

"And we all, who with unveiled faces contemplate **the Lord's glory,** are being transformed into his image with ever-increasing glory, which comes from the Lord, who is the Spirit" (2 Corinthians 3:18). Father God, I decide to stop concentrating on myself, on my weaknesses, my failures and even on my efforts to improve. I take my eyes off these things and begin to contemplate the glory of Your beloved Son, Jesus Christ. You transform me into His image by Your Spirit. I realise this doesn't happen by my strength or effort, but by Your Spirit (Zechariah 4:6). Thank You for Your Spirit who lives in me.

"For God, who said, 'Let light shine out of darkness', made his light shine in our hearts to give us the light of **the knowledge of**

God's glory displayed in the face of Christ" (2 Corinthians 4:6). My heavenly Father, You know how much I long to know You, to know Your glory. You tell me that Your glory shines in the face of Your precious Son, Jesus Christ. Like the Psalmist, my heart insists that I seek Your face (Psalm 27:8). I choose to seek Your face and I know that I will be completely satisfied.

"Whom I created **for my glory**, whom I formed and made" (Isaiah 43:7). Heavenly Father, I praise and thank You for creating me for Your glory. Just as You created the fish to live in the water, You created me to live in Your glory. I choose to live in Your glory and be one with You. IT'S ALL ABOUT YOU, LORD!